MARY MOTHER OF GOD

MARY MOTHER OF GOD

Her Life in Icons and Scripture

EDITED BY GIOVANNA PARRAVICINI

TRANSLATED BY PETER HEINEGG

Liguori/Triumph
LIGUORI, MISSOURI

Imprimi Potest:
Richard Thibodeau, C.Ss.R.
Provincial, Denver Province
The Redemptorists

Published by Liguori/Triumph
An imprint of Liguori Publications
Liguori, Missouri
www.liguori.org

Translation copyright 2004 by Liguori Publications

Previously published under the title *Vita di Maria in Icone*, copyright 2001, Edizioni San Paolo, Piazza Soncino, 5-20092 Cinisello Balsamo (Milano).

Library of Congress Cataloging-in-Publication Data

Vita di Maria in icone. English.
    Mary, Mother of God : her life in icons and scripture / edited by Giovanna Parravicini ; translated by Peter Heinegg.
        p. cm.
    ISBN 0-7648-1211-4
    1. Mary, Bessed Virgin, Saint—Art. 2. Icons, Russian. 3. Mary, Blessed Virgin, Saint—Biography. I. Parravicini, Giovanna.
II. Title.

N8189.3M35V5813   2004
755'.55'0947—dc22   2004048847

Printed in Italy
08 07 06 05 04   5 4 3 2 1
First U.S. edition 2004

CONTENTS

INTRODUCTION

A Spiritual Reading of the Icons of Mary

"If anyone asks you about your faith, take him to church and show him the icons." This advice from Saint John Chrysostom puts icons in their native context, in the place of honor, the iconostasis, and in the liturgy where they are venerated, incensed, and prayed to. Or else icons look down from the "angle of beauty," usually on a little altar adorned with flowers and lights, in houses and even in the humblest peasant huts. "Praying is necessary for the painter who paints the image, praying is requested of the faithful standing before the icon, praying is indispensable for all the Church."[1] Only in this atmosphere do icons become a place where God meets with human beings.

The contents of the icons are undoubtedly *dogmatic*, as the teaching of the Eastern Church makes clear. The Second Council of Nicea (A.D. 787) spells this out vis-à-vis the iconoclasts, who, inflamed by the ancient Docetist heresy, raged against the icons of Christ and the *Theotokos*. The council affirmed that icons are legitimate because if the Son of God truly became incarnate in the virginal womb of Mary, he may be depicted in art.

But the function of the icons is primarily *spiritual*, insofar as they put us in touch with the prototypes that they represent. They are *guiding* images (P. Evdokimov), because they lead us from the material signs to the persons shown, from the visible to the invisible, from time to glorious eternity. Thus, Marian icons aim at creating an encounter not so much with a historical personage who lived in distant times, as with the living and glorified person of Mary, who helps the faithful to find salvation.

To enter more intimately into the secret of icons, including those of Mary, it is not enough to reflect theologically on iconology in general[2] or on Marian iconology in particular.[3] We need prayerful contemplation.

Theology underlines the *eschatological* character of the icon as an "image of the world to come" (P. Florenski) and its *anthropological* character, according to which the *Theotokos* appears as "the image of spiritual perfection." As T. Spidlik explains, Christ is *the one who is to come* (*ho erkhómenos*) for whom "every faithful soul, the entire Church, indeed the whole earth, the whole cosmos, must prolong in history the *fiat* of the Virgin of Nazareth."[4] The Incarnation is reproduced in the new life of the believer, so that all Christians become like Mary "the mother-virgin" (Maximus the Confessor). For this reason, Mariology cannot be independent, but "remains an intrinsic part of the whole Christian teaching as an anthropological leitmotiv" (V. Losski).

Hence the true icon of Mary is not the naturalistic or Renaissance one that depicts her as a beautiful woman with a marvelous baby, but the one that manifests her mystery, that is, the one that leads Christians to the knowledge and love of the Son, the Spirit, and the Father. The epiphanic character of the *Theotokos* is mediated through a *typology*, which doesn't so much establish the features or profile or portrait,[5] so much as the various types of her representation: *Hodigitria* or guide to Christ, who is the way; *Eléousa* or the tender and merciful one, who holds in her arms the Child who clings affectionately to his Mother, cheek to cheek; *Orante*, representing the Virgin standing by Jesus' side (*Déesis*) or with hands raised and with the Child on her lap framed in a circle (*Platítera*); *Galaktotrofousa* or nursing mother, which represents Mary with the Child at the breast and *Kyriottissa* or queen enthroned in the costume of *Basilissa* or empress.

But it's not enough to know all this in theory. One needs to personally take on the posture of readiness in the face of the icons. It is neither necessary nor possible to leave one's own environment and enter the Eastern churches. Even a book like this one, which you now hold in your hands, can be a help, because it presents you with thirty-nine typical Marian icons, accompanied by an excellent selection of texts from the Bible and the Fathers of the Church.

It has been edited with intelligence and love by Giovanna Parravicini, an iconographer who is well versed in the artistic and spiritual process of the icons. The choice, naturally, doesn't follow an abstract or systematic criterion, but one that emerges from the history of salvation. One moves from the Old to the New Testament to highlight the life of Mary or rather of the presence of the *Theotokos* in the mysteries of salvation that are concentrated in Christ. She is present above all in the waiting for salvation by the people of Israel, as a new Eve, the burning bush, the closed door, a stone, Gideon's fleece. Then comes the sequence of the mysteries of Christ that are realized in history and in which Mary is present or that concern her on the first level: Mary's conception, her birth, her presentation in the temple, the Annunciation, the Nativity, Jesus' presentation in the temple, his public life, the Crucifixion and Ascension of Jesus, Pentecost, and finally Mary's dormition.

Through the icons and the texts accompanying them we seem to see the realization of an authentic *mystagogy* or initiation into the mysteries. While our eyes rest on the representation, the inspired words of Andrew of Crete or the Sicilian Joseph the Iconographer and of so many Fathers help us to penetrate into the salvific events and to perceive the deep significance of the presence of the *Theotokos* in the life of Christ and of the Church. Mary is greeted as "most precious treasure of the earth, immaculate dove, inextinguishable lamp" (Cyril of Alexandria). It takes no more than this exercise of contemplation—should there be any need of it—to reconcile the rationalistic West to the figure of Mary. With this in mind, Vladimir Ivanov voices the wish: "Mariology is the theology of the future, free from the interference of intellectualism."[6]

But don't think that a simple contemplation is enough to realize the encounter with the salvific persons and realities. One needs the "light of Mount Tabor," which helps men and women to rediscover the riches and the meaning of the mystery, one needs the Spirit to introduce one to the secret of the icon: "The icon is a place of the Spirit, a point of the cosmos where the Spirit is present to grant us access to what the icon expresses" (Father Gabriel, monk of St. Nicholas).

So let whoever takes this book in hand invoke the Holy Spirit to walk the *Via Pulchritudinis* recommended by Paul VI at the International Marian Congress of 1975. This is the "path open to all, even to simple souls: it is the *path of beauty*, the path to which we are led, in the end, by the miraculous, marvelous, and stupendous teaching that makes up the theme of the Marian Congress: Mary and the Holy Spirit. In fact, Mary is the creature who is '*tota pulchra*': she is the '*speculum sine macula*'; she is the Woman 'clothed with the sun' (Rev 12:1), in whom the purest rays of human beauty meet with the sovereign, but accessible rays of supernatural beauty."[7]

Stefano de Flores

Notes

1. T. Spidlik, "*Teologia dell'iconografia mariana*," in *La Madre del Signore* (Bologna, 1982), p. 247.

2. The following works are distinguished, theologically speaking: N. P. Kondakov, *Ikonografia Bogomateri*, 2 vols. (St. Petersburg, 1914), a work of synthesis, the result of travels and research that has remained unmatched to this day; E. Trubetskoy, *Contemplazione nel colore: tre studi sull'icona russa* (Milan, 1977), written in Russian between 1915 and 1917; L. Ouspensky, *Essai sur la théolgie de l'icône dans l'Église orthodoxe* (1960); P. Evdokimov, *La teologia della bellezza*, 6th edition (Milan: Cinisello Balsamo, 1996).

3. M. Donadeo, *Icone della Madre di Dio* (Brescia, 1982); A. Quacquarelli, F. Bisconti, "*L'iconologia mariana antenicena e i suoi presupposti*," in S. Felici, ed., *La mariologia nella catechesi dei padri (età prenicena)* (Rome, 1989), pp. 241–256; G. Gharib, *Le icone mariane: Storia e culto*, 2nd ed. (Rome, 1988); E. Sendler, *Le icone bizantine della Madre di Dio* (Milan: Cinisello Balsamo, 1995).

4. T. Spidlik, *op. cit.*, pp. 243–254.

5. The profile of Mary is sketched by Nicephorus Callistus (fourteenth century) and by the *Ermeneutica della pittura* by Dionisio di Furnà (d. c.1745), republished in Naples in 1971.

6. *La Madonna a Mosca e a Roma: Teologia, arte, devozione popolare* (Milan: Cinisello Balsamo, 1992), p. 35.

7. Paul VI, *Discorso per la chiusura del VII Congresso internazionale mariologico e l'inizio del XIV Congresso internazionale mariano* (Rome, May 16, 1975).

PART I
MARY IN THE OLD TESTAMENT

ONE

MARY AS THE NEW EVE

Throughout the universe the cry is heard
of those who celebrate today's feast in unison.
Death came because of a man;
but because of a man salvation came as well.
The first man fell into sin;
the second man lifted up the one who had fallen.
Woman defends us from woman,
the first one opened the path to sin;
the second prompted the entrance to justification.
The first followed the serpent's counsel,
the second presented the serpent's killer,
and brought forth the author of light.
The former, by means of wood, introduced sin.
The latter, in contrast, also by means of wood, introduced good.
By wood I mean the cross;
and the fruit of this wood is always green
and becomes immortal life for those who taste it.

Gregory of Nyssa, *Homily on the Birth of Christ*, in *Testi mariani del primo millennio*
(henceforth referred to as "TM"), 4 vols, (Rome: Città Nuova, 1, 317)

The Last Judgment (page 5) depicts the Second Coming of Christ, around whose throne the whole creation revolves. He is crowned by the humanity of the Old and New Testaments: Adam and Eve, the Mother of God, and John the Baptist, united by the Redemption (the serpent, which is licking Adam's heel, no longer has any power).

"The Last
Judgment"
(Detail: "The
'New and the
Old' Creatures
Before the
Throne of the
Most High"),
1580–1590,
School of
Stroganov.

TWO

PRAISE FOR THE MOTHER OF GOD

Jacob left Beer-sheba and went toward Haran. He came to a certain place and stayed there for the night, because the sun had set. Taking one of the stones of the place, he put it under his head and lay down in that place.

And he dreamed that there was a ladder set up on the earth, the top of it reaching to heaven; and the angels of God were ascending and descending on it.

And the LORD stood beside him and said, "I am the LORD, the God of Abraham your father and the God of Isaac; the land on which you lie I will give to you and to your offspring; and your offspring shall be like the dust of the earth, and you shall spread abroad to the west and to the east and to the north and to the south; and all the families of the earth shall be blessed in you and in your offspring. Know that I am with you and will keep you wherever you go, and will bring you back to this land; for I will not leave you until I have done what I have promised you."

Then Jacob woke from his sleep and said, "Surely the LORD is in this place— and I did not know it!" And he was afraid, and said, "How awesome is this place! This is none other than the house of God, and this is the gate of heaven."

Genesis 28:10–17

THE LORD WENT IN FRONT OF THEM in a pillar of cloud by day, to lead them along the way, and in a pillar of fire by night. Neither the pillar of cloud by day nor the pillar of fire by night left its place in front of the people.

Exodus 13:21–22

FROM THE WILDERNESS OF SIN the whole congregation of the Israelites journeyed by stages, as the LORD commanded. They camped at Rephidim, but there was no water for the people to drink.

The people quarreled with Moses, and said, "Give us water to drink." Moses said to them, "Why do you quarrel with me? Why do you test the LORD?" But the people thirsted there for water; and the people complained against Moses and said, "Why did you bring us out of Egypt, to kill us and our children and livestock with thirst?"

So Moses cried out to the LORD, "What shall I do with this people? They are almost ready to stone me."

The LORD said to Moses, "Go on ahead of the people, and take some of the elders of Israel with you; take in your hand the staff with which you struck the Nile, and go. I will be standing there in front of you on the rock at Horeb. Strike the rock, and water will come out of it, so that the people may drink." Moses did so, in the sight of the elders of Israel. He called the place Massah and Meribah, because the Israelites quarreled and tested the LORD, saying, "Is the LORD among us or not?"

Exodus 17:1–7

ON THE MORNING OF THE THIRD DAY there was thunder and lightning, as well as a thick cloud on the mountain, and a blast of a trumpet so loud that all the people who were in the camp trembled.

Moses brought the people out of the camp to meet God. They took their stand at the foot of the mountain. Now Mount Sinai was wrapped in smoke, because the LORD had descended upon it in fire; the smoke went up like the smoke of a kiln, while the whole mountain shook violently. As the blast of the trumpet grew louder and louder, Moses would speak and God would answer him in thunder.

Exodus 19:16–19

HAIL, HOLY MOUNTAIN, on which God set foot; hail, spiritual bush unconsumed by the flames; hail, sole bridge that lets mortals pass from the world to eternal life. Hail, pure and uncontaminated Virgin, who brought forth the salvation of our souls! Jacob saw you prophetically as a ladder, O Mother of God, because for your sake the Most High God appeared on earth and willed to speak with men, the blessed and glorious God of the Fathers. [...]

Singing of your Son, we all celebrate you as a living temple, O Mother of God; because, having dwelt in your womb, he who bears up all things in his hands made you holy, made you glorious. [...]

Hail, O Rock who quenched those who thirst for life! Hail, O Pillar of fire who guided those in darkness; O Shelter of the world, wider than the clouds. Hail, O Land of the promised good. Hail, you who flow with milk and honey. Hail, O Bride and maiden ever pure.

Akathist Hymn, TM, 1, 960

The tradition of this orthographic type (page 9) takes us back to Mount Athos, where a miraculous icon of the Mother of God was kept that dripped balm (myron). The Virgin is represented here at the center of the painting, framed by a garland of flowers, which winds its way around her and opens into a second, smaller oval above that, from which Christ-Emmanuel appears, giving his blessing. The Mother of God is presented this way as the promised flower that blossomed amid her people to give birth to the flower of the earth, Jesus Christ. She is set among the patriarchs and Old Testament prophets who in one way or another preannounced the saving event, and now praise the Virgin with the words of their prophecies, written on the scrolls they bear in their hands.

On the left, beginning at the top, we see Habakkuk, Jeremiah, Aaron, Moses, and David; on the right, Ezekiel, Jacob, Gideon, Daniel, Isaiah. Each one of the Fathers holds a symbol that at once characterizes the life of the saint and is a prophecy of the Virgin (Moses has the burning bush, David the ark of the covenant, and so on). At the feet of the Virgin, we see the kneeling figure of Balaam, the pagan seer who blessed Israel and prophesied the star of the Messiah.

The painter of the icon doesn't stop at representing the prophetic attributes and the related inscriptions: the tender green tonality of the background and the ornamental floral motifs accentuate the importance and symbolic expressiveness of the spring flowers, of the invisible growth, of the seeds of grains, grasses, and flowers. This image is directly linked to the texts of the prophecies that are read on the feasts dedicated to the Mother of God and to the Nativity of Christ: "Instead of the thorn shall come up the cypress; instead of the brier shall come up the myrtle; and it shall be to the LORD for a memorial, for an everlasting sign that shall not be cut off."[1] These images are also bound up with the verse from the Song of Songs: "I am a rose of Sharon, a lily of the valleys,"[2] which in the exegesis of ancient and modern theologians refers to the renewal of the earth and the marriage of the Church with Christ, its heavenly spouse. In the icon, the allusion to the spousal union between the Church as Mother of God and Christ is visible in the intertwining garlands of blue flowers that surround the two figures and that recall the nuptial ornaments beloved in the mid-East in ancient times.

1. Isaiah 55:13
2. Song of Songs 2:1

*"Praise for the
Mother of God
With the
Akathist Hymn,"
middle of the
sixteenth
century,
Moscow.*

RUSSIAN MUSEUM,
ST. PETERSBURG

9

The nineteenth-century icon (page 11) keeps the freshness of the chromatic tonalities—based in this case on roseate tones—that also relate to light and to springtime blossoming, but that allude in addition to the color of blood and the passion. The overall structure of the composition is also maintained, which sees the garland of the Virgin and on high the Savior Emmanuel giving his blessing; but the host of the prophets thickens because of the "encyclopedic" taste that characterizes later icons. If, on the one hand, the representation of the attributes of each prophet is less pronounced, their identification is scrupulously attended to through their names, which can be seen on their halos, and the cartouches with the prophetic text that each one of them holds in his hands.

*"Praise to the
Mother of God
in the Akathist
Hymn,"
eighteenth
century,
Russian icon.*

PRIVATE COLLECTION, ITALY

THREE

The Mother of God As the Burning Bush

Moses was keeping the flock of his father-in-law Jethro, the priest of Midian; he led his flock beyond the wilderness, and came to Horeb, the mountain of God. There the angel of the LORD appeared to him in a flame of fire out of a bush; he looked, and the bush was blazing, yet it was not consumed. Then Moses said, "I must turn aside and look at this great sign, and see why the bush is not burned up." When the LORD saw that he had turned aside to see, God called to him out of the bush, "Moses, Moses!" And he said, "Here I am." Then he said, "Come no closer! Remove the sandals from your feet, for the place on which you are standing is holy ground." He said further, "I am the God of your father, the God of Abraham, the God of Isaac, and the God of Jacob." And Moses hid his face, for he was afraid to look at God.

Then the LORD said, "I have observed the misery of my people who are in Egypt; I have heard their cry on account of their taskmasters. Indeed, I know their sufferings, and I have come down to deliver them from the Egyptians, and to bring them up out of that land to a good and broad land, a land flowing with milk and honey."

Exodus 3:1–8

THEN THE GLORY OF THE LORD went out from the threshold of the house and stopped above the cherubim. The cherubim lifted up their wings and rose up from the earth in my sight as they went out with the wheels beside them. They stopped at the entrance of the east gate of the house of the LORD; and the glory of the God of Israel was above them.

Ezekiel 10:18–19

THE PROPHECIES CONCERNING YOU have been fulfilled, O chaste Virgin! A prophet prefigures you as the gate of Eden turned toward the East, through which no one passed except the Maker of you and of all the universe.[1] Another saw you as a bush engulfed in flames:[2] the flames, in fact, of the deity took up residence in you and did not consume you. Another described you as the holy mountain from which broke loose, without human intervention, the cornerstone[3] that struck the statue of the spiritual Nebuchadnezzar. Truly great and paradoxical is the mystery fulfilled in you, O Mother of God! Therefore we glorify you: through you, in fact, salvation came to our souls.

The Red Sea once prefigured the image of the Spouse who did not know the experience of cohabitation. Then Moses divided the waters;[4] now Gabriel is the mediator of the wonder.[5] Then Israel traversed the abyss with dry feet, now the Virgin gives birth to the Christ without seed. After the passage of Israel, the sea remained impassible; after the birth of Emmanuel, the Immaculate One remained incorrupt. O you who are, who were, and have appeared as man, have mercy on us!

You are the temple and gate, palace and throne of the King, O Virgin most August! For you my Redeemer, Christ the Lord, appeared to those who lay in darkness.[6] He who is the sun of justice, wished in this way to illuminate those whom he had created in his image[7] with his own hand. Therefore, O worthy of all praise, who has acquired with him the boldness of a mother, pray to him incessantly that he may save our souls.

John Damascene, Dogmatic Writings on the Theotokos, TM, 2, 546

1. See Ezekiel 44:2
2. See Exodus 3:2
3. See Daniel 2:31
4. See Exodus 14:21
5. See Luke 1:26
6. See Luke 1:79
7. See Genesis 2:7

The biblical episode in which God appears to Moses gave rise to a particular icon of the Mother of God, which establishes a rather rich and complex link between the New Testament and the Old Testament prophecies that announce the coming of salvation through Mary.

The Mother of God stands out in the center of the icon (page 15) on the eight-pointed star, which indicates the presence of the Lord of Hosts, the Ancient of Days, and alludes to the bush (the four blue rays), which burns in the fire of the divine energy (the red rays).

The focus is on the regal nature of the Virgin. The Queen of Heaven surrounded by the angelic hosts, by the symbols of the Evangelists (in the red rays), and by the natural elements that obey her will. According to the visions of the Book of Revelation, the angelic choirs are represented with their particular attributes (stars, clouds, lightning bolts, torches, swords) as dispensers of the natural elements. At the four corners of the picture, Moses is shown facing the burning bush (in the upper left); on the lower left, Ezekiel stands before the closed door of the sanctuary, to signify the Virgin by whom Christ will be brought forth; in the upper right, we see the seraph who purifies the lips of the prophet Isaiah with the burning coal. Finally, on the lower right, Jacob wrestles with the angel.[1] The central depiction of the Mother of God also has a prophetic content: we can see the symbols of the stairway (which after the Incarnation rejoins heaven and earth), of the rock (prophecy of Daniel), and the representation of Christ as the High Priest, who celebrates the Eucharist on the altar of his tomb, in Jerusalem.

1. Genesis 32:23–33

*"The Mother of
God As the
Burning Bush,"*
*end of the
eighteenth
century,
Russian icon.*
PRIVATE COLLECTION, ITALY

15

"The Mother of God As the 'Burning Bush,'" sixteenth century, Monastery of Solovki.

DISTRICT MUSEUM OF
KOLOMENSKOYE, MOSCOW

FOUR

THE MOTHER OF GOD AS SIGN

Again the LORD spoke to Ahaz, saying, Ask a sign of the LORD your God; let it be deep as Sheol or high as heaven. But Ahaz said, I will not ask, and I will not put the LORD to the test. Then Isaiah said: 'Hear then, O house of David! Is it too little for you to weary mortals, that you weary my God also? Therefore the Lord himself will give you a sign. Look, the young woman is with child and shall bear a son, and shall name him Immanuel. He shall eat curds and honey by the time he knows how to refuse the evil and choose the good.'"

Isaiah 7:10–15

LISTEN TO ISAIAH WHO PROCLAIMS: "A child has been born for us; a son given to us."[1] Learn from the same prophet how the child has been born, how a son has been given. In conformity with the law of nature perhaps? The prophet denies it. The master of nature does not obey the laws of nature. But how was the child born? Tell me. The prophet answers: "Look, the young woman is with child and shall bear a son, and shall name him Immanuel"[2] which translated means: God-with-us. […]

It seems to me that the great Moses had already known this mystery through the light in which God appeared to him when he saw the bush burn without being consumed.[3] Moses actually said: "I wish to draw nearer to see this great vision." I believe that by the term "draw nearer" he did not wish to indicate a movement in space, but a drawing near in time. What was truly prefigured in the flame and in the bush, once the time in between had passed, was openly manifested in the mystery of the Virgin.

As the bush burned on the mountain, but was not consumed, so the Virgin gave birth to the light and was not corrupted. Let not the comparison seem inappropriate to you: the bush prefigures the body of the Virgin, which has given birth to God.

Gregory of Nyssa, Homily on the Birth of Christ, TM, 1, 317

---

1. Isaiah 9:6   2. Isaiah 7:14   3. Exodus 3:1

"Our Lady of the Sign," middle of the sixteenth century, central Russia.

STATE MUSEUM OF
THE HISTORY OF MOSCOW

The typology of the Mother of God of the Sign is the most solemn; it is a "full-length" variant of the ancient "Orante," generally placed in the apse immediately beneath the representation of the Pantocrator. In this typology (page 18), in fact, the Virgin stands for the Church, which receives in itself the Incarnate Word and reveals it to humanity. This solemn event is alluded to by the presence of the Seraphim alongside Mary, who represent the angelic hosts in the sight of the deity.

Represented frontally, the Virgin lifts her hands in the gesture of prayer, of supplication, and shows on her breast the effigy of Christ-Emmanuel, that is, not the Jesus of the Gospels, but the Logos who exists before time and history and who is announced by the prophets: "The Lord himself will give you a sign. Look, the young woman is with child and shall bear a son, and shall name him Immanuel," God-with-us.[1]

The arms and the hem of the mantle of the Mother of God ideally delineate the outlines of a chalice in which Christ offers himself in sacrifice for the salvation of humanity. The lineaments of the face of Emmanuel are not those of an infant, but of an adult and kingly man; and the gestures of his hands (the blessing that he imparts with the right and the scroll of the law that he clutches in his left) underline his divine humanity.

1. Isaiah 7:14

*"Our Lady
of the Sign
With the Holy
Patron of the
Commissioner,"
seventeenth
century.*
MUSEUM OF ART, HISTORY, AND
ARCHITECTURE, SERGEYEV POSAD

MARY, THE NEW ZION

Now the angel of the Lord came and sat under the oak at Ophrah, which belonged to Joash the Abiezrite, as his son Gideon was beating out wheat in the wine press, to hide it from the Midianites. The angel of the LORD appeared to him and said to him, "The LORD is with you, you mighty warrior." Gideon answered him, "But sir, if the LORD is with us, why then has all this happened to us? And where are all his wonderful deeds that our ancestors recounted to us, saying, 'Did not the LORD bring us up from Egypt?' But now the LORD has cast us off, and given us into the hand of Midian."

Then the LORD turned to him and said, "Go in this might of yours and deliver Israel from the hand of Midian; I hereby commission you." He responded, "But sir, how can I deliver Israel? My clan is the weakest in Manasseh, and I am the least in my family." The LORD said to him, "But I will be with you, and you shall strike down the Midianites, every one of them." […] Then Gideon said to God, "In order to see whether you will deliver Israel by my hand, as you have said, I am going to lay a fleece of wool on the threshing floor; if there is dew on the fleece alone, and it is dry on all the ground, then I shall know that you will deliver Israel by my hand, as you have said." And it was so. When he rose early next morning and squeezed the fleece, he wrung enough dew from the fleece to fill a bowl with water. Then Gideon said to God, "Do not let your anger burn against me, let me speak one more time; let me, please, make trial with the fleece just once more; let it be dry only on the fleece, and on all the ground let there be dew." And God did so that night. It was dry on the fleece only, and on all the ground there was dew.

Judges 6:11–16, 36–40

"YOU WERE LOOKING, O KING, AND LO! There was a great statue. This statue was huge, its brilliance extraordinary; it was standing before you, and its appearance was frightening. The head of that statue was of fine gold, its chest and arms of silver, its middle and thighs of bronze, its legs of iron, its feet partly of iron and partly of clay. As you looked on, a stone was cut out, not by human hands, and

*Detail of "The
Mother of God,
'The Stone
Not Broken
Off by Human
Hand,'" early
seventeenth
century,
School of
Stroganov.*
MUSEUM OF SOLVYECHEGODSK

22

it struck the statue on its feet of iron and clay and broke them in pieces. Then the iron, the clay, the bronze, the silver, and the gold, were all broken in pieces and became like the chaff of the summer threshing floors; and the wind carried them away, so that not a trace of them could be found. But the stone that struck the statue became a great mountain and filled the whole earth."

Daniel 2:31–35

HAIL, YOU WHO IN YOUR ENTRANCE into the Holy of Holies took a purple garment with which you had been truly clothed by God and placed it on us. In Eden, we had been stripped of the glorious covering that was not woven by human hands[1] because of the food that brought death and burned souls; you, O Spouse of God, who are the remission of sins[2] granted by God to us, filthy as we are with mud. Hail, you who today at the first beginning of the most splendid and venerable Presentation gathered together the whole host of the prophets who, with most beautifully sounding cymbals like harmonious instruments, intone the hymn of the most divine voice and lead the dance in joy to guide souls.

Hail, you who with the cadence of your steps trampled down the diabolical ser-pent with the tortuous mind, the hater of the good, who for men has been the wicked guide to disobedience:[3] you who took for companion on your path corrupt-ible nature, which had shown itself ready to fall, to bring it back once again toward the holy, immaterial tabernacle that knows not old age. Hail, you who with the torches of your Presentation made shine forth the day of joy and exultation[4] on those who were confined in the shadow of death and in the abyss of powerlessness, and guaranteed that God would decide to dissolve the darkness, O Mary most wondrous of all.

Hail, you who are the cloud[5] that sprinkles over us the divine spiritual dew,[6] you who with your entrance today into the Holy of Holies have made to rise the most splendid sun upon those who were kept in the shadow of death; fountain full of God, from whom flow the rivers of the knowledge of God, pouring the clearest gleaming water of orthodoxy, and destroying the mob of heresies.

Hail, most sweet and spiritual paradise, planted today toward the East by the omnipotent right hand of his will[7] and germinating unto him the fragrant lily and the rose that never withers [...], in which flowers the life-giving wood for the knowledge of the truth, from which those who taste become immortal. Hail, you who are the uncontaminated and most pure royal palace of God, the King of the universe, built in holiness, surrounded as you are by his majesty and generously restoring all of us with the mystic enjoyment of your self: you now are established in the dwelling of the Lord—and that is in his holy temple—while in you is found, truly embellished and not made by any human hand, the marriage bed of the spiritual spouse[8] and in you the Word, wishing to bring back on the road the wanderer, has joined in the flesh to reconcile[9] those who had already separated themselves by their own will.

Hail, new Zion and divine Jerusalem, holy "city of God the Great King, in whose towers God is made known,"[10] making kings bow down in veneration of your glory and disposing the whole world to celebrate in exultation the solemnity of your Presentation; you are truly the seven-branched candelabra,[11] golden and resplendent, lit by the timeless flame that is fed by the oil of purity and that guarantees the dawning of light upon those who are blinded by the gloomy darkness of sins. Hail, most fertile and shady mountain of God,[12] having been nourished in you, the spiritual lamb took upon himself our sins and infirmities; rolling down from the mountain, the rock not cut by human hands shattered the altars of the idols[13] and "became the cornerstone, a marvel in our eyes."[14]

Hail, you who are the holy throne of God, the divine offering, the house of glory, most beautiful splendor, chosen jewel, universal propitiation and "heaven that tells the glory of God."[15] East that makes a light dawn that does not set: whose "setting forth is from the end of the heavens, and outside whose warmth no one has ever been,"[16] that is, of ruling providence. Hail, you who with your birth have dissolved the chains of sterility, have melted down the curse of the Law,[17] have made blossom the blessing of grace, and who with your entrance into the Holy of Holies has brought to fulfillment the wish of your parents, the foundation of our pardon, and the fullness of our joy, since you have led before you the beginning of grace.

Hail, Mary, full of grace,[18] holier than the saints, higher than the heavens, more glorious than the cherubim, more honored than the seraphim, more venerable beyond all creation: you who with your glorious and splendid Presentation bring to us the olive branch that frees us from the spiritual flood,[19] or dove that brings us the joyful news of the port of salvation, and whose "wings are silver and whose back is the paleness of gold,"[20] which the most sacred and illuminating Spirit makes to shine; urn all of gold,[21] who contains the sweetness of our souls, Christ our manna.

Germanus of Constantinople, Homily I,
The Entrance of the Most Holy Mother of God, TM, 2, 328

1. See Genesis 3:17
2. See Ephesians 1:7
3. See Genesis 3:1–13
4. See Psalm 45:15
5. See Exodus 19:16
6. See Exodus 16:13
7. See Genesis 2:8
8. See Psalm 19:5–6
9. See Romans 5:10
10. See Psalm 48:3
11. See Exodus 25:31
12. See Psalm 68:16
13. See Daniel 2:34
14. See Psalm 118:22
15. See Psalm 19:1
16. See Psalm 97:11
17. See Galatians 3:13
18. See Luke 1:28
19. See Genesis 8:11
20. See Psalm 68:14
21. See Exodus 16:33

In this icon (page 27), a rare iconographic subject, the symbolism is closely connected to the prophecy of Daniel: "A rock broke off from the mountain, but not by the hand of man…and it became a great mountain that filled all that region." The rock that in Nebuchadnezzar's dream smashes to pieces the statue of the giant is Christ, while the Virgin is symbolized by the sky that sends down the rock. In fact, the mountain appears on the breast of the Mother of God, along with other symbols of Old Testament prophecies: the rainbow (sign of the alliance between God and humans), Gideon's fleece covered with dew, and Jacob's ladder, a symbol of the union of heaven and earth realized through the Incarnation. These symbolic representations are completed by the figure of Gabriel, who visits the Virgin for a second time, this time to announce to her the passion of her Son: this is alluded to by the cross, the lance, and the pincers that he shows to the Child and to his Mother.

"The Mother of God, 'The Stone Not Broken Off by Human Hand,'" early seventeenth century, School of Stroganov.

MUSEUM OF SOLVYCHEGODSK

PART II
MARY IN THE
NEW TESTAMENT

SIX

THE CONCEPTION OF MARY

A shoot shall come out from the stump of Jesse,
   and a branch shall grow out of his roots.
The spirit of the LORD shall rest on him,
   the spirit of wisdom and understanding,
the spirit of counsel and might,
   the spirit of knowledge and the fear of the LORD.

Isaiah 11:1–2

THE RIGHTEOUS FLOURISH like the palm tree,
   and grow like a cedar in Lebanon.
They are planted in the house of the LORD;
   they flourish in the courts of our God.
In old age they still produce fruit;
   they are always green and full of sap,
showing that the LORD is upright;
   he is my rock, and there is no unrighteousness in him.

Psalm 92:12–15

This complex composition *(page 33)* is inserted within an arch of several spans, which represents a sumptuous temple, a symbol of Paradise, in which grows the leafy tree of the genealogy of Christ. As fruits produced by this tree, on the branches appear the full-length figures of Christ's forebears, the prophets and just men who had prefigured his coming into the world. The trunk of the tree is made up of seven decorative medallions: on the lowest one, King David is depicted, sitting on a throne and intent on playing the psaltery; in the upper medallion, we see the Mother of God enthroned with the Child on her knees; in the five intermediary medallions are the kings of the line of David. From each medallion on the right and left originate branches, each made up in turn of six medallions, with full-length figures or scenes from the Gospels. Over each row of medallions, except for those above, are represented another twelve figures of ancestors of Christ and prophets with unrolled scrolls in their hands.

At the foot of the tree, as its root, on a green background we see the recumbent figure of the progenitor Jesse, David's father. But the genealogy of Christ goes back still further, all the way back to Abraham, as the artist indicates by placing on the lower branches the representations of him and his descendants, Isaac and Jacob.

Beneath the tree is shown a series of personages, the prophets and Sybils of antiquity, the philosophers and sages of the pagan world, to whom Christian literary critics and encyclopedists attributed sayings and testimonies about Jesus. Beyond that, the figures of the Christ's ancestors often alternate with persons not connected to him by bonds of blood. For example, on the highest branch on the right and left of the enthroned Mother of God, we can see Saint Joseph, Saint Ephrem, John the Baptist, and the old man Simeon. Lower down we can make out the prophet Isaiah, the three boys in the burning furnace, the prophet Daniel, and other Old Testament just persons. In this way, the icon represents a sort of exposition of the plan of salvation for the human race as developed by God, of the creation of the Christian church on earth, of whom the Virgin constitutes the first visible stone in the new alliance.

*"Tree of Jesse,"
1660–1670,
School of the
Palace of Arms,
Moscow.*

TRETYAKOV GALLERY, MOSCOW

SING AND REJOICE, O DAUGHTER ZION! For lo, I will come and dwell in your midst, says the LORD. Many nations shall join themselves to the LORD on that day, and shall be my people; and I will dwell in your midst. And you shall know that the LORD of hosts has sent me to you. The LORD will inherit Judah as his portion in the holy land, and will again choose Jerusalem. Be silent, all people, before the LORD; for he has roused himself from his holy dwelling.

Zechariah 2:10–13

AS ICE IN WATER OVERCOMES the liquid so long as night and darkness last, but then breaks up when exposed to the warm rays of the sun, so death ruled over man until the coming of Christ. But "when the grace of God our Savior appeared,"[1] and "the sun of justice"[2] rose, "death has been swallowed up in victory,"[3] no longer able to support the presence of the true life.

O abyss of the goodness and love of God for men! But in exchange for this infinite love we are not disposed to serve him. Instead of prostrating ourselves to adore his goodness, we put off searching for the reason why God came down among men.

O man, what shall we do? So long as God remains in heaven, you do not search for him. Now that he comes down toward you and lingers with you by means of his body, you are not disposed to welcome him, but seek out the reason why you have been able to become familiar with God. Learn, then, that God is in the flesh, because it was necessary that this flesh, already cursed, be sanctified; that this weakened flesh be strengthened; that this flesh which had become God's enemy be led back to friendship with God and this flesh that had fallen from paradise be taken back to heaven. And what is the workplace of this dispensation? The body of a Holy Virgin. And what are the active principles of this generation? The Holy Spirit and the overshadowing power of the Most High.

Basil the Great, *Homily on the Holy Generation of Christ*, TM, 1, 296

1. Titus 2:11
2. Malachi 4:2
3. 1 Corinthians 15:54

WHEN GOD CREATED MEN to do good, to know only Him and do his will, the devil was seized by envy. First of all, he sought to convince Adam to disobey by deceiving him by means of his wife Eve; then he convinced the other men to hold themselves far from God and to adore the soulless idols. Taking pity on his own creation, he gave the law and the prophets. But everything remained useless, and so he decided to send his own Son and Word to take on human form and free humans from the hand of the devil. To this end, he disposed the birth of her who would bear in her womb her Son, Mary the Immaculate Mother of God, from her holy parents Joachim and Anne, to whom God had promised, while they prayed, to give a fruit of the womb.

Menologion of Basilius II, TM, 2, 1043

HIS NAME WAS JOACHIM; he was of the house of David, king and prophet; his wife was called Anne. He remained childless until his old age, because his wife was barren. Yet especially for her, according to the law of Moses, had been prepared the honor of women who give birth, an honor that had not been given to any other woman without children. Joachim and Anne, in fact, were venerable and honorable both in words and deed. They were known as belonging to the line of Judah and David, to the pedigree of kings. When, therefore, the houses of Judah and Levi were united, the royal branch and the priestly branch were mingled. Thus, in fact, it is written with regard to both Joachim and Joseph, to whom the holy Virgin was betrothed. Of him, under the most immediate aspect, it is said that he was of the house and tribe of David:[1] but they were both, the two of them, one according to the natural descent from David, the one by virtue of the Law, of whom they were Levites. And blessed Anne too was a branch chosen from the same house: he foretold that the king who was about to be born from their daughter would be a high priest, because he would be God and man. [...]

The gracious king, the generous giver, received the prayer of the just Joachim and sent the announcement to both. He sent the announcement first of all to Joachim, as he stood in prayer in the temple. A voice was heard from heaven: "You will have a daughter who will be a glory not only for you, but for all the world." This announcement to Joachim was made known to the blessed Anne; she still did not cease to pray to God with burning tears. To her too was sent the announcement from God, in the garden where she was offering a sacrifice, with prayers and petitions. The angel of the Lord came to her and said: "God has heard your prayer; you will give birth to the announcer of joy. You will call her Mary, because from her shall be born salvation for the entire world." Now, after the announcement, the pregnancy took place, and Mary was born from the barren Anne, the woman who illuminates all: thus is translated the name "Mariam," "illuminatrix." Then the venerable parents of the blessed and holy maiden were filled with great joy. Joachim organized a banquet and invited all the neighbors, both the wise and the ignorant, and all gave thinks to God, who had performed a great prodigy. In this way, the anguish of Anne was turned into a more sublime glory, that of becoming the gate of God, gate of his life, and beginning of his glorious fulfillment.

Maximus the Confessor, *The Life of Mary*, TM, 2, 187–188

1. See Matthew 1:16, Luke 1:5

SHE HAS BEEN BUILT UP as the temple in which the Creator is to be received, a dwelling arranged for the Word who created all things, a cloud of light which wraps the Sun of justice. For the immortal Spouse a wedding bed of divine splendor is erected. He who wraps the sky with clouds prepares to make ready the divine appearance. He who intertwines the seasons with the climate and the coming years prepares for the wedding encounter.

Theodore the Studite, *On the Nativity of Our Lady, The Mother of God*, TM, 2, 640

O MARY, UNDEFILED, in your birth Joachim and Anne were freed from the reproach of childlessness, and Adam and Eve from the corruption of death. Indeed, your people celebrate being redeemed from the penalty of sins, and they cry to you: "The barren woman gives birth to the Mother of God, the nurse of our life."

Romanos the Melodist, *Canon on the Nativity of Mary*, TM, 1, 695

In this composition (page 39), the Virgin offers herself as a guide to Christ with her person (such is, in fact, the meaning of the Greek name of this Marian typology, in which Mary supports her Son on her arm, pointing to him with the other hand) and through the story of her vocation. On the frame, from the upper left, follow the scenes of her life, drawn from the Apocryphal and canonical Gospels. On the upper edge, in particular, are represented the stories of Joachim and Anne, who after years of sterility receive from the angel the announcement of the coming birth of a new creature. On the left appear the scenes of the two just persons in the temple, chased away by the priest because sterility was understood as a sign of divine disfavor. Two scenes follow in which Joachim is in the desert, whither he had fled to pray and do penance, and Anne in her rooms, are reached by the vision of an angel who announces to them the birth of a chosen creature. The final scene on the right represents the true and fitting conception of the Mother of God in the embrace of the two spouses who, against the background of the nuptial chamber, entrust to each other the words of hope received from the angel. Notice the red cloth that links the two buildings in the background, a symbol of the divine protection extended over humanity: God enters into human history to sanctify it and to build, through all its carnality, his alliance with the chosen people.

The term "of Smolensk" refers to the Russian city where the icon was located. Its veneration is bound up in particular with the invasion by the Tartars of Batuzh, who besieged the city in 1238 but were miraculously routed through the intercession of the Virgin. The feast of the icon is celebrated on June 28.

*"The Mother of
God: 'Hodigitria
of Smolensk,'
With Scenes
From Her Life,"*
sixteenth
century, School
of Moscow.

SEVEN

THE NATIVITY OF MARY

When the Lord stripped himself and then in a marvelous way took our form from us, we received the fullness and we were enriched by divinization, given to us in exchange for a lump of clay taken on by him. That is why all things exult today, and nature dances! "Let heaven rejoice on high and the clouds rain down justice, let the mountains drip sweetness, and let the hills exult, because the Lord had pity on his people, having raised up for us the throne of salvation of the house of David, his son,"[1] and that is this most immaculate Virgin, who knows not man, from whom Christ is born, the longing and salvation of the nations. Let every noble soul dance in chorus, and let nature call creation to its renewal and to its regeneration! […]

Let every creature lift up hymns, weave dances, and bring something worthy for this day! Let there be today a single communal celebration of heavenly and earthly beings; and let the entire concert of this world and the world beyond celebrate together as one. Today the sanctuary of the Creator of all things has been built; and in an extraordinary manner the creature is prepared for the Creator as his divine resting place. Nature, which previously had been brought down to earth, today receives the beginnings of its divinization; and dust hastens to run up toward the supreme glory. Today, Adam, who presents for us to God the first-fruits coming from God, offers Mary to him; and by means of her, the first fruits who of all the mix was not soaked with it, becomes bread for the regeneration of the race.

Andrew of Crete, Encomium I, *On the Birthday of the Most Holy Mother of God*, TM, 2, 396

1. See Luke 1:69, Isaiah 45:8, Joel 3:18, Amos 9:13

The composition of the Nativity of the Virgin (page 43) is formed in the Byzantine world on the basis of an apocryphal text, the Proto-Evangelium of James, to which the liturgical texts of the feast and the writings of the Fathers also go back. The fundamental scheme, which comprises the central scene of Anne on the bed, with the ladies rendering homage to her, and the bath of the newborn, goes back to the twelfth and thirteenth centuries, while the representation of Joachim and the cradle was added in the fourteenth century.

The vividness of the colors and the ornament, the rhythm of the dance in which the personages revolve around Anne and the Mother of God, reecho the tone of exultation that characterizes the feast. In particular, the presence of Déesis (Christ giving his blessing, with the angels and saints by his side, in a gesture of supplication) in the upper section underlines the providential level into which the event inserts itself, which represents the "beginning of our salvation."

"Birth of Mary, the Mother of God," first half of the fourteenth century, Pskov.
P. KORIN MUSEUM, MOSCOW

WHY WAS THE VIRGIN MARY BORN of a barren woman? Because it was necessary that for her, the only new thing under the sun,[1] at the peak of miracles, life was prepared with miracles, and gradually from the most humble realities greater ones would arise.

There is also another reason, more sublime and more divine. Nature, in fact, has been defeated by grace and has stopped, trembling, not enduring to be the first. When, therefore, the Virgin Mother of God was about to be born from Anne, nature did not dare to anticipate the budding of grace; but it remained sterile until nature made the fruit bloom. In fact, she who would bear the "firstborn of all creation, in which all things subsist"[2] [...] had to be firstborn herself.

Today is the beginning of the salvation of the world. "All the earth, acclaim the Lord, shout, exult, and sing for joy."[3] Make your voice heard; "raise it up, without fear,"[4] because in the holy Sheep Gate[5] the Mother of God has been born unto us, from whom the Lamb of God has deigned to be born, the Lamb who takes away all the sins of the world.

Leap for joy, mountains,[6] nature is endowed with reason and stretched toward the height of spiritual contemplation. Actually, the mountain of the Lord has sprung forth in all its splendor, which transcends and overtops every hill and every mountain, the height of angels and of men. From this, without a human hand, the cornerstone has deigned to break itself off, Christ the only Person who unites what is divided, divinity and humanity, angels and men, the pagans and Israel, according to the flesh in a single spiritual Israel.[7]

"Mountain of God, luxuriant mountain! Opulent mountain, luxuriant mountain, the mountain on which God has deigned to come down!"[8] [...] Peak more sacred than Sinai, covered not by haze nor by the storm nor the terrifying fire, but by the luminous ray of the Holy Spirit. There, in fact, the Logos of God, together with the Spirit, like a finger, wrote the law on tablets of stone; here, by the work of the Holy Spirit and her blood,[9] the Logos in person became flesh and offered himself to our nature as the most effective remedy of salvation. There manna: here he who gives the sweetness of manna.[10]

In the face of the living dwelling place, let the eminent dwelling place built by Moses in the desert with precious material of every sort bow down, and before that the one built by father Abraham. This did not accommodate the power of God, but really the person of the Son and God as well. Let the golden ark and the urn of gold in which were kept the manna and the candelabra and the table and all the objects of the ancient cults recognize that they are not comparable to her. They were honored as a prefiguring of this one, as shadows of the true prototype.

Today the Creator of the Universe, the divine Logos, has composed a new book, which the Father has poured out from the heart, so that it would be written with the tongues of God, the Spirit, as with a pen.[11] [...] O most holy little daughter of Joachim and Anne, you who escape the principalities and the powers, and the "fiery arrows of the Evil one";[12] you who lived in the marriage chamber of the Spirit and remained immaculate, to become the Spouse of God and Mother of God by nature! Most holy little daughter, who appeared in her mother's arms and threw terror into the rebellious powers! Daughter most holy, nursed at the breast and surrounded by angels! Daughter dear to God, glory of those who have given birth to you; generations upon generations will call you blessed, as you have truly affirmed! [...]

O Virgin, full of divine grace, holy temple of God, whom the spiritual Solomon, the Prince of peace, built and dwelt in, embellished not by gold, not by lifeless stones, but instead of gold, resplendent with the Spirit. In the place of precious stones, you have the inestimable pearl, Christ, the burning coal of divinity.

John Damascene, *Homily on the Birth of Mary*, TM, 2, 498

1. See Ecclesiastes 1:9
2. See Colossians 1:15
3. See Psalm 98:3–4
4. See Isaiah 40:9
5. Quarter in Jerusalem near the Temple, where, according to apocryphal tradition, Joachim and Anne lived.
6. See Psalm 114:4
7. See 1 Corinthians 10:18
8. See Psalm 68:15–16
9. See Luke 1:35
10. See Wisdom 16:21
11. See Psalm 45:1
12. Ephesians 6:16

In this icon (page 47), the story of the birth of the Mother of God is transformed into a solemn and joyous hymn of praise: the basic scheme is amplified though a series of episodes that are endowed with a profoundly symbolic significance, but that also express an intimate and lyric dimension. The author compares the dwelling of Joachim and Anne to a grand temple, and the walls, the atria, and the surrounding towerlike structures, to the holy city, Jerusalem, which in turn constitutes the archetype of the Church of Christ and of paradise. This is an illustration of the vision of the sanctuary of Jerusalem that God gave to the prophet Ezekiel: in fact, following the girl who goes up the steps we enter the internal atrium, then we come out under the portico, where the ministers of the temple met to bring vessels and gifts, and inside of which, like the sacrificial altar of the temple, appears the bed on which Anne is seated. Finally, above, in the place that in the temple was called the "hearth," and was considered "most holy,"[1] we see Joachim and Anne bent over the little Mary, "the animated and thinking ark of God." In the very construction of the icon, in the vertical thrust of the harmonious towerlike buildings, in the scansion of the spaces on more levels, the themes are developed of the building of the House of Wisdom, that is, of the working out of the divine plan of salvation for humanity, which is crowned by the divine redemption.

1. See Ezekiel 43:12–15

*"Nativity of the
Mother of God,"
final third of the
sixteenth
century,
Rostov?*
MUSEUM OF SERGEYEV POSAD

The Virgin is portrayed here (page 49), although in childlike proportions, in the arms of her mother Anne, already dressed as an adult: the purple mantle aims to underline the divine dignity that human, creaturely nature (symbolized by the blue tunic) takes on. The extremely fine gilded network on her mantle points to the presence of the divine.

As in the Child Jesus, we already have present here the fullness of humanity and divinity, so the vocation of the Child Mary is already fulfilled in the eyes of God. This is stressed by the presence of Christ blessing in the upper right corner: the mystery by which through the fiat of a creature, he who exists from all time, the true God, takes on flesh, is entirely present in the tender little creature whom Anne contemplates, aware that his birth has been willed from on high.

Representations of Saint Anne with the Child Mary are rather rare. This iconographic variant shows a tender scene between the mother and her baby, and underlines in particular the sweetness and intimacy of the composition, which repeats the scheme of the Mother of God of Tenderness, with the affectionate gesture of the Infant and the loving and afflicted glance of the Mother. In other cases, Mary is represented with a lily in her hand, resting on Anne's arm.

*"Saint Anne
With the Infant
Mary," middle of
the fourteenth
century, Serbia.*
MUSEUM OF THE TRINITY,
SERGIEV POSAD

EIGHT

THE PRESENTATION OF
MARY IN THE TEMPLE

The temple most pure of the savior,
the bridal-chamber most precious, the Virgin,
the sacred treasury of the glory of God
enters today into the Temple of the Lord,
bringing with her the grace of the Divine Spirit.
Therefore, the angels of God sing to her:
"This is the heavenly tabernacle!"

[…] The Redeemer, Word of the Most High, having decided to make himself
seen in the flesh for us, caused the Virgin to appear on earth, granting to the Most
Immaculate One an extraordinary origin and marvelous growth. He gave her in
fact as the fruit of prayer after having announced her in advance to the just Joachim
and Anne. Her parents received that Chaste One as a sign of faith, promising to
offer her to the Lord with joy and love. She is the super-celestial tabernacle.

The Chaste One thus having been born by divine providence, the just ones, as
promised, took her to the Creator in the temple. Then, Anne, visibly at the height
of joy, said to the priest: "Receive her, and lead her within to the sacred things of
the Lord, and guard her. She was given to me as a blessing, and I promised to bring
her with joy to him with faith. This one is the super-celestial tabernacle."

George the Hymnist, *Kondakion for the Presentation of Mary in the Temple*, TM, 2, 300

*"Presentation of
the Mother of
God in the
Temple,"
nineteenth
century,
Palech.*
PRIVATE COLLECTION, ITALY

ADDRESS OF GREETING OF ZECHARIAH TO THE CHILD MARY: Come here, little girl, loftier than the heavens. Come here, you who are seen as a child and who are known as the divine workshop. Come here, sanctify still more the vestibule of the sanctuary; in fact, to put it briefly, you have not been sanctified, rather you are the one who greatly sanctifies it.

Come here, make your way to the penetralium and toward the cell that stirs up trembling, you who shall become an immense and inscrutable treasure. Enter into the vestibule of the altar, you who tread upon the vestibule of death. Look within, toward the veil,[1] you who with your brightness illuminate those who have been blinded by darkened inclinations. Stretch forth your hands to me, who leads you like a little child. Take my hand: I am weary with old age; I have given in to the transgression of your commandment out of earthly ardor; lead me to life. See, I hold you like a little staff of old age, restorer of nature weakened by the fall. Behold, I see you, who will become the support of those who have fallen toward death. Come near to venerate the table, which, it has often been said, was a prophecy of you, most spiritual and uncontaminated table. Walk across the whole enclosure of the altar, because, breathing the odor of incense,[2] you have become more than perfume for those who breathe its fragrance, you who won distinction by being proclaimed the thurible of the language inspired by God, and of the prophets who were bearers of the Spirit.

Arise, arise on the staircase of the sacred dwelling. Pleased by the freshness of your beauty, the daughters of Jerusalem joyously weave your praises, and the kings of the earth will declare you blessed: you who have been recognized as the divine foundation and in the sweetest way pointed out to Jacob, the patriarch par excellence, as the ladder supported by God.[3] Come, O Lady, because leaning on such a pedestal is appropriate for you who are [...] a throne higher than the cherubim. Behold, since you are queen of the universe, I have worthily attributed to you the first seat; but you yourself raise up those who have plunged down. And hence now together with David I cry: "Hear, O daughter, consider and incline your ear; forget your people and your father's house, and the king will desire your beauty."[4]

The old man behaved this way, even though he would have liked to lavish more words of praise than these. The parents moved on, and their daughter, consecrated to God, was left behind. Trembling, the angels served her with victuals; and the girl was fed by immaterial beings with nourishment—whether material or immaterial we know not. Thus, through an intervention from God, the rites of divine initiation were carried out; thus, the child grew and gained strength, while the harm of the curse inflicted on us in Eden grew weaker.

Germanus of Constantinople, *Homily I on the Entrance of the Most Holy Mother of God into the Temple*, TM, 2, 327–328

1. See Exodus 26:31
2. See Exodus 30:1
3. See Genesis 28:12
4. Psalm 45:10–11

This icon (page 57) represents in its details the story of the life and the calling of Mary, focusing on the central mystery of the Annunciation and already prefiguring the birth of Jesus (this is alluded to by the presence of a dark cave at the feet of the Virgin, where we read: "Jesus Christ willed to be born in the cave"), but developing in particular the theme of her childhood. The higher section of the bordering vignettes are dedicated to the conception of the Mother of God, then follow the scenes of her birth, of the blessing of the priests (the three characters who stretch their hands toward Mary, who is in Joachim's arms), and a few scenes of a more intimate and familial character: the Virgin fussed over by her parents and taking her first steps between the two of them.

The icon scenes that follow have as their background the temple, in which, according to the Apocrypha, Mary was taken at the age of three years. In the scene of her presentation at the temple (page 59), which is laconic and essential in its lines, there are, however, comprised all the essential elements of the narrative: the high priest receives Mary, accompanied by her parents who offer her to God with an anxious and sorrowful gesture (Anne lays a hand on her cheek in the attitude of the Mother of Sorrows), while against the background appear some figures that point to the procession of virgins that he had introduced into the sacred place. Up high, the scene of the angel who nurtures Mary during her stay in the Temple.

The Prayer of the Rods (page 60) alludes to the episode of the choice of a husband for Mary, reported by the Apocrypha. The holiness of the Virgin shines through in the iconographic composition from various elements: during the prayer of the high priest, the rods turn toward the Mother of God, within the sanctuary, and the priest himself prays with his arms extended toward her.

"The Annunciation With Scenes From the Life of Mary, the Mother of God," 1580–1590, School of Stroganov.

MUSEUM OF HISTORY AND ART OF SOLVYCHEGODSK

WHAT WAS THE VIRGIN DOING as she spent her life within the confines of the Holy of Holies? She received from the angels the food of the angels and kept her virginity intact, like an immaculate dove. She gave thanks and manifested a most profound affection for him who had built the Temple, heavens, and the earth, as she said in her supplication: "Oh all-powerful Lord, I will praise you who wiped away the opprobrium of Eve, the first Mother, and through your ineffable mercy you will send to the earth your Only-Begotten Son, to live amid human beings. It is for this reason that I shall render his dwelling pure and immaculate." [...]

What name, then, shall we give to Mary?

Heaven? She contained in her womb the Creator of heaven and earth.

Sun? She, who shines seven times more brightly than the sun, has conceived the Sun of justice.

Moon? She, who is resplendent with incomparable beauty, has brought forth Christ, the essence of all beauty.

Cloud? She bore in her arms him who is clothed in clouds.

Candelabrum? She glowed like light for those who sit in darkness and the shadow of death.

Throne? She in the Holy Spirit had received, circumscribed within her bosom, him who reigns invisibly on the throne of the Father.

Pearl? She has given to mortals a pearl by far the most precious.

Paradise? In opening the gates of Eden to those who were condemned, she continuously gains them entrance into an eternal realm.

Mountain? She bore without difficulty him who touches the mountains and they smoke.[1]

Earth? She bore within her womb without pain him at whose sign the earth shakes.

Altar? She nourished with her motherly milk him who gives us food in abundance.

Sea? She kissed with her lips him who gathered the waters into one place only.

Tarasius of Constantinople, *Homily on the Presentation of Mary in the Temple*, TM, 2, 634

1. See Psalm 104:32

*A detail
of "The
Annunciation
With Scenes
From the Life
of Mary, the
Mother of God":
Presentation of
Mary at the
Temple, 1580–
1590, School of
Stroganov.*

A detail from
"The Annun-
ciation With
Scenes From the
Life of Mary, the
Mother of God":
Prayer of the
Rods, 1580–
1590, School of
Stroganov.

NINE

THE ANNUNCIATION

Today has arrived the joy of all people, the joy that undoes the ancestral condemnation. Today has arrived the one who is everywhere, he who fills all things with joy. Not having bodyguards, not leading with him troops of angels, not exalting his march, but in silence and tranquillity. He did this to remain hidden from the prince of darkness and to trap the serpent with prudent artifice. […] His compassion for us, infinitely great, would not allow so great a work to go to ruin, that is, man, for whom he had set up the heavens in the form of a vault,[1] and solidified the earth, had poured forth the air, had laid out the sea, and had built all of animate creation.

For this reason the God borne in the womb of the Virgin is the God on earth, the God in heaven, the God among men, the God who is everywhere and who is not contained by these things. Hence, the nature of man is given the prelude of joy, and receives the beginning of divinization. Hence, having been stripped of the fallacious riches of sin, she is led to the Creator as his spouse. Hence, our first creation receives a new one, and the aged world puts away the aging derived from sin. But let the heavens above rejoice, and clouds rain down justice. Let the mountains distill honey and the hills "be girt" with jubilation, because God has had pity on his people.[2] In fact, today the "mystery hidden for centuries"[3] has been revealed, and "all things receive their recapitulation in Christ."[4] Today the supreme creative authority of the universe lends its counsel to conclusion, meditated on before the creation of things, to reject the counsel premeditated by the author of malignity against us from the very beginning. For this reason, the angels exult, and together with them, men make glad, and the whole world returns to itself, turning back.

God sent Gabriel to Nazareth. "Go then to Nazareth, city of Galilee. Having arrived there, immediately and first of all direct this message to the Virgin, that is, the glad announcement of the joy that was first destroyed by Eve; but do not disturb her mind! Since the announcement is of joy and not ruin, the greeting is of joyfulness and not sadness." Indeed, for the human race what joy was able or would ever be able to be more glad than this, that is, the joy of becoming a participant in the divine nature and, through the conjunction with him, becoming a single thing with him with regard to unity and hence to the hypostasis? And what could be more stupefying for us than to see God's condescension: he goes all the way to being conceived in the bosom of a woman? O incredible things! God amid the limbs of a woman, "he who has his throne in the heavens and his footstool on the earth,"[5] God is contained in a womb, he who is above the heavens and dwells together with the eternity of the Father! And what could be more unbelievable than this, to see God in human form, without deviating from his own divinity? To see human nature bound up with its Creator so that man, who first fell into sin, may be completely divinized?

Andrew of Crete, *Homily on the Annunciation of
the Most Holy Mother of God*, TM, 2, 413

1. See Isaiah 40:12
2. See Isaiah 45:8, Amos 9:13, Psalm 65:13
3. See Ephesians 3:9
4. See Ephesians 1:9
5. See Isaiah 66:1

This delicate composition (page 63) expresses above all the quivering, highly emotional homage paid by the archangel to the Virgin Mary in the texts of the feast, which the Eastern Church celebrates as one of the main solemnities of the liturgical year: the Mother of God is seated on a throne, at her shoulders, the building of the temple and the red banner of divine protection, upon her descends the tripartite ray of divine grace. The angel indicates with his gesture and bow his veneration for the "inviolate Spouse." The garments of the Mother of God and the cushions on which she sits are red and blue, the colors of humanity and divinity; her attitude is not one of surprise or of fear, but of total receptivity to the Word who is made flesh within her.

The tender springtime colors of the icon, the delicate scintillation of the silvery coating of the backgrounds underline the meaning of the rebirth of the feast of the Annunciation: March 25 was, as a matter of fact, considered to mark the beginning of the world, the date of Creation.

*"The
Annunciation,"
fifteenth century,
School of
Novgorod.*
MUSEUM OF NOVGOROD

TODAY THE ETERNAL MYSTERY IS REVEALED as the Son of God becomes the Son of man. By sharing in the lesser he enables us to share in what is greater. Of old, Adam sought to be God, and failed; now God becomes man to make Adam God. Let all creation thrill with joy, as the archangel appears before the Virgin, for his greeting signals the end of our sorrow.[1] Our God! From compassion you became man. Glory to you.

Theophane the Writer, *Troparion for the Feast of the Annunciation*, TM, 2, 678

1. See Luke 1:28

This monumental work (page 65) faithfully takes up again the oldest icon of the Annunciation preserved in Russia, the work of a Byzantine master from the twelfth century (Tretyakov Gallery, Moscow). The composition particularly stresses the solemnity of the event through the richness of the gold on the wings and the clothing of the archangel, through the almost immobile pose of the personages: Gabriel with his arm raised in the gesture of greeting, and the Virgin with her head lightly reclined in the gesture of assent. In this icon they are caught, not at the moment of the Annunciation, but in the tremulous veneration of the mystery that has taken place, through the power of God, who is seated on high in the heaven segment: in the bosom of the Virgin we see in fact the profile of the Infant, whose body is already taking shape. (This is the metaphorical significance of the skein of red thread that Mary has in her hand; as Saint John Damascene says, the King of glory, having become incarnate and entered the world by means of the Virgin "is clothed with the purple of his flesh.")

The scenes on the edge from the Akathist hymn (literally "the hymn that is chanted standing up"), dedicated to the Virgin who had saved the city of Constantinople from assault by its enemies, describe the event of the Annunciation in the story of the salvation of humanity; and they function as "prayers in color" to this particularly venerated image (it was the patron-icon of the Cathedral of the Annunciation in the Kremlin in Moscow, the palace chapel of the tsars).

*"The
Annunciation
With Scenes
From the
Akathist Hymn,"*
*first half of the
seventeenth
century,
Moscow.*
CATHEDRAL OF THE
ANNUNCIATION, MOSCOW

ODE V: *The Theotokos:* How can the Inaccessible One, invisible to all, dwell in the womb of a Virgin created by himself? How will she be able to conceive God, the Word coeternal with the Father and the Spirit?

The angel: When he promised to his ancestor David to place on the throne of his kingdom a fruit of his loins,[1] God chose only you, a beauty of Jacob, for a spiritual dwelling place.

ODE VI: *The Theotokos:* O Gabriel, receiving the glad sound of your words, I am filled with divine joy: you truly reveal joy and you announced unspeakable joy.

The angel: To you, O Mother of God, was given the divine joy. To you, O Spouse of God, all creation cries out, "Hail!" You alone, in fact, O Pure One, were predestined to be mother of the Son of God.

The Theotokos: And so let the sentence of Eve be annihilated through me; let the ancient promise be restored completely by means of me.

The angel: God had promised to Father Abraham, O Pure One, to bless all nations in your seed. Today through you the promise finds fulfillment.

ODE VII: *The Theotokos:* Announcing that immaterial light, through immense compassion, is about to unite with the matter of the body—splendid announcement, divine proclamation!—now to me you exclaim: Blessed, O All Pure One, is the fruit of thy womb![2]

The angel: Hail, Queen! Hail, Queen most pure! Hail, receptacle of God! Hail, lamp of light, recall of Adam, rescue of Eve, holy mountain, illustrious sanctuary and nuptial chamber of immortality.

The Theotokos: The coming of the Most Holy Spirit has purified my soul, sanctified my body, making of me a vast temple of God, an embroidered tent, an animated sanctuary, and chaste mother of life.

The angel: I contemplate in you a lamp with many flames, a bedchamber built by God. And now, like the ark of gold, receive the author of the Law, O Immaculate One, who was pleased by means of you to save the perishing nature of men.

Theophane, Canon for the Annunciation, TM, 2, 682

1. See Psalm 132:11
2. See Luke 1:41

TEN

THE BIRTH OF JESUS

What shall we offer you, O Christ,
you who for our sake became man on earth?
Every creature of yours gives you thanks:
the angels offer you song,
the sky its stars, the Magi gifts, the shepherds their astonishment at the miracle,
the earth a cave, the desert a manger;
and we offer you a virgin mother. [...]
Let heaven and earth prophetically rejoice,
let angels and men spiritually exult:
God has indeed appeared in the flesh
to those who were sitting in darkness and the shadow of death.
A crib and a manger received the one born of the Virgin:
the shepherds announce the miracle,
the Magi from the East bring gifts to Bethlehem.
We too with pure lips, like the angels of God, offer praise:
glory in heaven to God and peace on earth,
since the longing of the nations has been fulfilled.

John Damascene, *Stichera on the Birth of Christ*

The composition (page 69) poetically illustrates the text of the verses of Saint John Damascene, "What shall we offer you, O Christ…": The Mother of God, celebrated by all creatures, is seated on the throne and holds the Christ Child on her knees before her. Her throne, surrounded by a round mandorla made of three concentric circles, which symbolizes the Trinitarian life and moves from a tender azure to nuances of golden rose, leans on the top of a rocky mountain, toward which converge mountain ranges crowned with steep peaks. At the top, the composition is crowned by a dark blue rainbow, against the background of which figures of angels can be seen on their knees. On the left, the Magi approach with their gifts; on the right, there is symmetrically placed a group of three young shepherds. Still symmetrically, below at the foot of the throne are represented allegorical female figures; on the left the Earth, which points to the cave offered by her as a gift to Christ; on the right the figure of the Desert, which proffers to the Mother of God the stone manger. Both the cave and the manger are symbols of the future death and resurrection of Christ: the one reminds us of the infernal abyss into which Christ will descend to bind Satan and liberate the just, the other refers to the tomb within which his body will be placed after death.

The group of men dressed in festive garments depicted below in the center of the composition, flanked by two personages in monastic dress, symbolize humanity, which sings the praises of the Virgin (in Byzantine iconography, the unusual pointed hats mark the category of the singers). The two monks are John Damascene (on the left) and Cosmas of Maiama (on the right), author of some of the most famous Marian hymns. The icon constitutes a sort of pictorial "poem," which through the representative figures hymns the mystery of the divine maternity.

*"Synaxis of
the Mother of
God,"* first half
of the fifteenth
century, Tver.
P. KORIN MUSEUM, MOSCOW

HERE WE HAVE THE LORD. Here we have the manger. Through this a divine mystery is revealed to us; namely, that the gentiles—living like dumb beasts in a stable—would be fed in abundance by sacred nourishment [...]. These signs by which God is recognized are by no means to be disparaged: signs such as ministering angels, Magi coming to adore, and martyrs bearing witness. He emerges from the womb, but comes like lightning from the heavens. His bed is a lonely stable, but the Child glows in light. A married lady gives him birth, but a Virgin conceived him. A wife conceived, but a Virgin brought him forth.

Ambrose of Milan, *Exposition of the Gospel of Luke*, Book 2, TM, 3, 187

THE VIRGIN TODAY gives birth to the Sovereign One,
and the earth offers the cave to the Inaccessible One.
Angels with the shepherds sing songs of praise;
the Magi journey with the star to guide their way.
For us there has been born
a newborn Babe,[1]
the God before time.[2]

Bethlehem opened Eden, come let us behold. We have found delight in this hidden place; come let us take the pleasures of Paradise within the cave. There appeared an unwatered root which sprouted forgiveness, from which David once yearned to drink;[3] and there the Virgin brought forth an infant who at once quenched their thirst, that of Adam and David. Come, then, let us hasten to this place where there has been born a newborn Babe, the God before time. [...]

When the blameless virgin saw the Magi carrying in their hands the new and shining gifts, and kneeling before him, and when she saw the shepherds singing hymns and the star clearly revealing him, she entreated the One who is creator and Lord of all, saying: "Receive the three gifts, my child, and grant three prayers for her who gave you birth. I beg you on behalf of the heavens above and the fruits of the earth, that those who dwell thereon, be reconciled to all for my sake, since you have been born a newborn Babe, the God before time.

"For I am not simply your mother, O merciful savior, nor is it without prearranged plan that I give milk to you, the giver of milk. But I beg you on behalf of all human beings. You have made me the pride and boast of all my race. For your universe considers me as a powerful protection, rampart, and stay. May those who were cast from the joys of Paradise look to me that I may direct them to a perception of all things. Grant this for me who gave birth to you, a newborn Babe, the God before time.

"Save the world, Savior. For its sake you came. Establish your kingdom. For its sake you have let your light shine on me and the Magi and all creation. Lo, the Magi, on whom you have allowed the light of your countenance to shine, are falling down before you, and they bring you gifts of gold, beautiful things, much sought after. I have need of them, since I am about to go to Egypt, and flee with you, for you, my Guide, my Son, my Maker, my Redeemer, and newborn Babe, the God before time."

Romanos the Melodist, Hymn I for the Birth of Christ, TM, 1, 704

1. See Isaiah 9:6
2. See Psalm 90:2
3. See 1 Chronicle 11:17

MARY, GOING TO THE CRIB, bows her head and entreats her son as she says: "My son, since you have exalted[1] me through your condescension, my poor race, through me, now beseeches you. For Adam, crying bitterly, came to me, and Eve joined him in his laments. The serpent is the cause of this; he stripped them of their honor. Therefore, they are begging to be clothed, as they cry to me: 'Mary, full of grace.'"

As soon as the immaculate one brought these petitions to the God lying in the cradle, at once he received them and subscribed to the writing of the prophets. He says: "O mother, I save them because of you and through you. Had I not willed to save them I should not have dwelt in you. I should not have allowed my light to shine from you, and you would not have heard yourself called my mother. It is for your race that I lie in the crib. At my will I now give milk to your breasts. You bear me in your arms for their sake. The cherubim do not see me, but you behold me, and carry me and cherish me as son, Mary, full of grace."

Romanos the Melodist, Hymn II for the Birth of Christ, TM, 1, 711

1. See Luke 1:49

In Christian tradition, after the feast of Easter, the second commemoration of Christ was the Theophany, the "manifestation of the God-man." The feast goes back to the fourth century, in Rome, around A.D. 380, the celebration of the Nativity (which at that time recalled different events of the Gospel: the adoration of the Magi, the baptism of Christ, and the marriage feast at Cana) was introduced at Constantinople by Saint Gregory Nazianzen. At around the same time, the first ecumenical councils elaborated the Christological dogmas that found their definitive expression in the Nicene Creed.

The liturgical and theological evolution is reflected in Christian art: the icon (page 73) inspired in fact by sacred Scripture and the liturgy. The first (the narrative of the Gospel of Luke) provides the particulars of the historical event and points out in realistic language the circumstances of the birth of Jesus in Bethlehem. Further scenes can be made out: in the center, the Virgin and the cave with the Infant,[1] on the right the appearance of the angel to the shepherds,[2] in the upper left the journey of the Magi following the star.[3] Scenes from the lower strip are taken from the Apocryphal gospels: the conversation of Joseph with a personage that tradition identities with the Tempter, and the bathing of the newborn Jesus, which alludes to purification and baptism.

The liturgy of the feast is characterized by exultation and awe for the prodigy that is taking place, which the icon expresses through the dancing rhythm and the revolving movement of the scenes, which stop, however, at the center, where the Mother of God, immersed in a motionless atmosphere, meditates in recollection upon the wonder. The Child, wrapped in swaddling clothes, which recall a winding sheet, already prefigures the dramatic destiny that awaits him, for the salvation of the human race.

1. See Luke 2:6–7
2. See Luke 2:8–15
3. See Luke 2:16–20

*"The Birth of
Jesus," middle
of the sixteenth
century,
Moscow.*
RUSSIAN MUSEUM,
ST. PETERSBURG

"I, THE CREATOR OF THE UNIVERSE, have taken you as mother. And, as a child, I grow—perfect, from you—without stain. I am swathed in swaddling clothes for the sake of those who long ago wore covering of skin.[1] The cave is beloved by me for the sake of those who hated the pleasure of paradise, and loved corruption, and transgressed my life-bearing command. I came down to earth in order that they might have incorruptible life.[2] [...]

"I am conquered by the loving concern that I have for human beings. [...] You will see me, the babe whom you carry in your hands, with his hands nailed to the cross in a short while, because I love your race. The one to whom you give milk, others will cause to drink gall. The one whom you call 'life,' you shall see hanging on a cross, and you shall weep for him as dead; but you shall greet me risen, Mary, full of grace."

Romanos the Melodist, *Hymn II for the Birth of Jesus*, TM, 1, 711

1. See Genesis 3:21
2. See Genesis 10:10

In this composition (page 75) the dramatic significance of the Birth of Christ, already present in the typical representation of the Byzantine tradition, is accentuated by means of the detailed account, on the one side, of the Magi, of their meeting with Herod and the angel's warning not to return to him, and, on the other, through the dream of Joseph and the flight to Egypt. In this way, the mystery of Christmas becomes the prefiguring of the manifestation of Christ to the gentiles (the adoration of the Magi) and of his passion (the slaughter of the innocents and the flight into Egypt).

*"The Birth of
Jesus," c.1660,
Moscow.*
ANDREI RUBLÉV MUSEUM

ELEVEN

THE PRESENTATION OF JESUS IN THE TEMPLE

He who is borne aloft by the Cherubim and sung by the Seraphim is today borne into God's temple according to the law, and is placed in the arms of the old man as if on an altar. From Joseph he receives gifts pleasing to God: a pair of turtle doves as a sign of the immaculate Church and a new chosen people of the gentiles, and two small young doves symbolizing the old and the new alliance. Simeon, as he welcomes the fulfillment of the promises, blessing the Virgin Mary, Mother of God, preannounces in her the signs of the passion. He asks the Lord to be discharged, saying: "Lord, now lettest thou thy servant depart in peace, for mine eyes have seen thy salvation, Lord and Savior of the Christian people."

Andrew of Crete, *Great Vespers*

I SALUTE YOU, O MARY, Mother of God, Virgin Mother, bearer of the Light, uncontaminated vessel. I salute you, O Virgin Mary, mother and servant, Virgin, by means of him who was born from you; mother by means of him who was wrapped in your swaddling clothes and whom you nourished with your milk; servant, through whom he took on the form of a servant. [...] I salute you, O Mary, temple who received God, or rather holy temple, as the prophet David exclaims, when he says, "Holy is your temple, marvelous in justice."[1]

I salute you, O Mary, most precious treasure of the earth; I salute you, O Mary, immaculate dove; I salute you, O Mary, inextinguishable lamp. From you, in fact, was born the Sun of justice. [...]

I salute you, O Mary, Mother of God, through whom entered into the world the true light, Our Lord Jesus Christ, who says in the Gospel, "I am the light of the world."[2] I salute you, O Mary Mother of God, through whom the light came down on all who were in the darkness and the shadow of death. "The people who walked in darkness have seen a great light."[3] And what light is that if not Our Lord Jesus Christ, the true light that enlightens every man who comes into this world?

Cyril of Alexandria, Homily XI, TM, 1, 491

1. Psalm 64:4–5
2. John 8:12
3. Isaiah 9:2

This icon (page 79), which belongs to the festive series painted by the Rublëv workshop for the Cathedral of the Dormition in Vladimir, is distinguished by its intimacy and sweetness, by the long and emotional contemplation expressed in the glances of those present, and especially in the gesture of Simeon. The old man holds in his arms the child Jesus and contemplates him with a consuming sweetness, holding him right up to his face—all in an instant that borders on infinity. In the background behind him, the ciborium and the altar insert the encounter into the history of salvation, alluding to the victim immolated and to the eucharistic sacrifice: old Simeon in fact is the symbol of the celebrant who lifts in his hand the sacred gifts in order to place them on the altar.

The Virgin, associated with the passion of Christ, participates here in this liturgical celebration in front of the altar, lifting her veiled hands as a sign of veneration for the mystery: she is the symbol of the Church, which makes Christ present in the eucharistic sacrament and in the communion of the believers. The Church is also represented here through the two figures on the side, Saint Joseph and the prophetess Anna, his glances converge toward the central focus of the composition, the tiny figure of Christ. The composition is thus characterized by a profound and peaceful equilibrium, in which emotion dissolves in an adoring contemplation.

*"Presentation
of Jesus in the
Temple," 1408,
Andrei Rublëv,
Daniel Chorny,
and assistants.*
RUSSIAN MUSEUM,
ST. PETERSBURG

LET THE CLOUDS SEND DOWN RAIN: in fact, Christ, like the sun carried by a light cloud, rests as a boy on pure arms in the temple. Let us acclaim him, then, O faithful: "Let us sing to the Lord, because he is covered with glory!"

Recover your strength, hands of Simeon, now weakened by old age; and you tottering knees of the old man run straight to Christ. Together with the choirs of the incorporeal, we sing to the Lord, because he is covered with glory.

Heavens established with intelligence, exult! And you, earth, be glad! Your Maker, indeed, the Christ, who is in the bosom of God, is led as a child to God the Father by the Virgin Mother, he who exists from before all ages. He has indeed covered himself in glory. [...]

One time on Mount Sinai, Moses saw the back of God[1] and was made worthy to hear in a confused fashion the voice of God in the darkness and storm; now Simeon receives in his arms God who has taken flesh for us even while remaining unchangeable, and gladly hastens to pass from this life to life eternal. For this cry out: "Now let thy servant go, O Lord."[2] [...]

Contemplating the Word without beginning in the flesh, borne by the Virgin as on a throne of Cherubim, Simeon cries out to him in wonder: "All things are full of your praise!"

When Isaiah saw an image of God in glory seated on a high throne, accompanied by angels, he exclaimed: "Oh wretched me, I have foreseen the God of the light that does not set, the Lord of peace!"

The divine old man, seeing the Word carried in the arms of the Mother, understanding the glory that had manifested itself one time to the prophet, exclaims: "Venerable lady! Like a throne you bear the God of light without setting, and Lord of peace! Your loving kindness, O Christ, covers the heavens: you have truly gone forth from the temple of an intact mother, so as to appear in the temple of your glory, like an Infant, sustained in arms, and you have filled all things with your praise."

Bending down, the old man kisses with divine transport the footprints of the Mother of God who has never known nuptials: "You bright fire, O Chaste One," he exclaims. "I tremble to receive in my arms this little boy who is the God of light without setting, and Lord of peace!"

"Isaiah was terrified when he received the burning coal from the seraph!"[3] cries the old man to the Mother of God. You dazzle me by handing to me him whom you bear, the light without setting and Lord of peace!" [...]

Let us turn to the Virgin to see her Son carried to Simeon; the incorporeal spirits, contemplating from heaven, say in amazement: "Let us now contemplate wondrous and glorious, incomprehensible, unspeakable things. He who created Adam is carried like an infant; the ungraspable is hugged in the arms of the old man, the uncircumscribed in the bosom of the Father is voluntarily circumscribed in the flesh, not in divinity, O only friend of man."

Cosmas of Maiuma, *Canon for the Feast of the Presentation in the Temple*, TM, 2, 601–603

1. See Exodus 33:23
2. Luke 2:29
3. See Isaiah 6:6

FROM THE WORDS OF SIMEON, "And a sword will pierce through your own soul too,"[1] some believed that the Mother of the Lord would die as a martyr (pierced by the stroke of a sword). But that is not how it was. In fact, the sword fashioned by a blacksmith may divide a body, but it cannot cut the soul; for which reason the Virgin too remains immortal by means of the one who dwelt in her, he who, taking her along with him brought her to the heavenly dwelling places. What, then, does Simeon mean when he says to the Virgin: "...so that thoughts out of many hearts may be revealed (and a sword will pierce through your own soul also)"? With these words, namely that the sword would pierce her soul, Simeon wished to signify the pain of the Virgin, that she would suffer, believing she had lost him who came to seek all those who were dead. [...]

Simeon, looking to the future, foretold this sorrow as a sword that cut through the soul, and said to the Virgin: "A sword will pierce your soul." But he did not say: "A sword will conquer," or "A sword will win out," but a sword will pierce through. By this he meant: "You, O Virgin, will be pained and afflicted for a time, but soon you will be set free from your pain."

Timothy of Jerusalem, *Homily on Simeon*, TM, 2, 46

1. Luke 2:35

This ancient painting (page 83) was probably part of a diptych with the representation of the dead Christ (Imago Pietatis). The face of the Virgin is sorrowful and afflicted. Her hands—which are arrestingly drawn—convulsively seize her breast, as if she were next to the cross. Nevertheless, the art of the Christian East always expresses the fullness of the Christian mystery: in this case, the affliction of the Virgin is serene, humble, subject to the divine will because she is aware of the ultimate truth, represented by the resurrection.

In her maternal sorrow, the Virgin does not cease being before all else the Mother of the Church who intercedes with Christ for humanity wounded by sin. The pain of the Virgin is the pain of the Church, who gives birth to a new humanity in weeping. The expression on her face is like the aspect of the Virgin in the presentation in the temple when she contemplates the Christ Child in the arms of Simeon, and she listens to his prophecy: wrapped in dark, almost monastic, garments, the splendor of the Mother of God is all internal, entrusted to the luminosity of the face and the hands, to the look of the sad and deep eyes to which no pain, no loneliness, no human cross, is alien. The pain here is completely redeemed, lived in the light of the Christ present and risen, even as the glory of Christ is based on the cross and is the continuous memory of it.

"The Sorrowful Mother of God," end of the thirteenth century, Byzantine.

TRETYAKOV GALLERY, MOSCOW

TWELVE

MARY IN THE PUBLIC LIFE OF CHRIST

The all-holy and immaculate Mother was there also, an eyewitness of the miracles and also listening to the teaching of the Lord. The mediatrix of all good things was the mediatrix of this miracle, too, because, as immaculate Mother, she desired to see the signs of her Son and Lord. For this reason, with respect and prudence, she drew his attention, and without giving him an order to do a miracle, nevertheless discreetly let him know the need of the moment, saying: "They have no wine."[1] From the depth of her heart she wanted to see the miracle take place, because she knew that he was the creator of all things, he who renews and changes nature as he wishes, he who had dwelt in her bosom in a manner superior to the laws of nature, keeping incorrupt her virginity: and he had gone forth from her bosom as he had wished, keeping her womb sealed and intact. Hence she had understood that he could do all that he wanted. [...]

Thus the most holy Virgin Mother of the Lord, as far as possible, stayed inseparably united with her sweet Lord and desired Son. She accompanied him wherever he went and thought of it as salvation and the light of her eyes and of her soul to be able to journey with him and to listen to his words. [...]

While the Lord came and went, as he announced and proclaimed salvation and healed every sickness and alienation, the pious ladies often accompanied him, and served him, witnessing the miracles he performed, as is written in the Gospel: "There were many women who followed Jesus from Galilee, and they served him."[2] But the holy and glorious Mother of the Lord was the guide of all of them, their protection and mediatrix with her Son and Lord. [...]

Thus, there is transmitted to us, and we repeat it, that after the ineffable birth which transcends all knowledge, even that of the immaculate and blessed Mother, the Virgin-Mother never separated herself from her beloved Son and King; ever since childhood he was her Lord. She nursed him as she should have, served him as a handmaid, and remained inseparably united to him. When he reached the age of twelve years, and they went up to Jerusalem for the feast of Passover and upon returning the boy Jesus stayed behind in Jerusalem, the immaculate Mother went about searching for him with anguish and sighs. And when she found him, she asked him sorrowfully: "Son, what have you done to us?" and what follows. Then he returned with them and came to Nazareth, and the royal Lord of all things remained subject to them. Then, when thirty years had been fulfilled, he began his apostolate and was baptized by John in the Jordan; and the Holy Spirit came over him in the form of a dove, and the Father attested from heaven that he was his beloved Son, and he began to preach and perform miracles. The holy Mother always accompanied him when she could [...] and listened to his teachings.

Maximus the Confessor, Life of Mary, TM, 2, 236

1. John 2:3
2. See Luke 23:55

O YOU, WHO BY YOUR POWER changed water into wine,
Change into the joy the affliction
    of the sins that oppress me,
Through the mediation of the Mother of God,
    O Christ, God,
Who has created all things in your wisdom.

[...] The Master spoke out clearly to the servants, "Draw the wine which was not harvested, and after that, offer drink to the guests. Replenish the dry cups. Let all the crowd and the bridegroom himself enjoy it;[1] for I have in marvelous fashion given pleasure to all; I who have in wisdom created all things."

When Christ, as sign of his power, changed the water into wine, all the crowd rejoiced, for they considered the taste marvelous. Now we all partake at the banquet in the church, for Christ's blood is changed into wine and we drink it with holy joy, praising the great bridegroom, the Son of Mary, the Word before all time who took the form of a servant, he who has in wisdom created all things.

Romanos the Melodist, Hymn for the Wedding Feast at Cana, TM, 1, 718

1. See John 2:6–8

The composition (page 87) is linked to the parable of the wedding guests, and forms part of the cycle of miracles and Gospel parables that unfolds in the cross vaults of the church of the Nativity of the Virgin. The marriage feast at Cana[1] represents the first miracle of Christ, where for the first time he reveals his divine nature and the significance of the salvation that he brings. According to the traditional interpretations, each gospel guest can be understood not only as a eucharistic archetype, but also as a figure of the future blessedness of Paradise prepared for the just; still more, this reading relates in particular to the wedding guests. Then, too, the final words of the Gospel story on the marriage at Cana, about the good wine that the host saves until the end of the banquet, echo the words pronounced by Christ during the Last Supper about the "new wine" that he would drink together with his disciples in the "kingdom of my Father." Finally, the wine served at the end of the banquet is a symbol that is close to the meaning of the oil in the lamps in the parable of the wise and foolish virgins[2] or to the wedding garment that the wedding guest lacks. All these symbols express the idea of the endless interior preparation that is required of man in view of the Last Judgment, of the definitive encounter with his Lord.

The Virgin, who stands out in the center of the fresco, is the figure of the "Disciple," who awaits the manifestation of Christ and believes in his divine humanity.

1. John 2:11
2. Matthew 25:1–13

*"The Wedding
Feast at Cana,"
1502–1503,
fresco.*

CHURCH OF THE NATIVITY OF THE
MOTHER OF GOD IN THE
MONASTERY OF FERAPONT,
PROVINCE OF VOLOGDA

GOD, THE SON OF GOD, entered into the womb of the all-holy Virgin and, taking flesh from her and becoming man was born—as we said—perfect God and perfect man. He is the same who is both without confusion. Now, pay attention! What thing greater has ever happened for us? All of us who believe in the same Son of God and Son of the ever-Virgin *Theotokos*, Mary, and who, believing, receive the word concerning him faithfully in our hearts. When we confess him with our mouths and repent our former lawlessness from the depths of our souls, then immediately—just as God, the Word of the Father, entered into the Virgin's womb—even so do we receive the Word in us, as a kind of seed, while we are being taught the faith. Be amazed on hearing of this dreadful mystery, and welcome this word, worthy of acceptance, with all assurance and faith.

We do not, of course, conceive him bodily, as did the Virgin and *Theotokos*, but in a way which is at once spiritual and substantial. And that One whom the pure Virgin conceived we possess in our hearts, as Saint Paul says: "God who called the light to shine from the darkness, has shone in our hearts to give us the light of the knowledge of his Son" (2 Cor 4:6).

[…] My intention in writing is that his genuine and infinite love be made manifest, and that, according to the divine word of our Lord Jesus Christ, if we desire it, all of us, too, may receive in the manner described, the title of his brothers [and sisters] and become the equals of his disciples and apostles—not, indeed, by becoming the latter's equals in worthiness, nor by accomplishing the missions and labors which they sustained, but by the action of God's own grace and gift which he has richly poured out on all who will to believe in, and to follow him without turning back. This is just what he so clearly desires when he says: "My mother and my brothers are those who hear the word of God and do it" (Lk 8:21).

Simeon, the New Theologian, *Tract I on Ethics*, TM, 2, 1037

"Vladimir Madonna of Tenderness, With Scenes From the Akathist Hymn," sixteenth century, Moscow.
DISTRICT MUSEUM OF VLADIMIR

"*Mother of God*" *(Theotokos in Greek) is the title that the Council of Ephesus in* A.D. *431 attributes to the Madonna, and that Eastern tradition has kept and preferred through the centuries until today. The icon of the Mother of God (page 89) expresses above all the mystery of the divine maternity. The Virgin is caught as the Son, embracing her tenderly, reveals to her his passion. Sweet, tender, sad, joyous, penetrating, understanding, Mary subsumes in herself the fiat of the entire Church, pronouncing it in the name of all creatures.*

The prototype of this typology comes from Byzantium (tradition holds that it was painted by the evangelist Luke). It was given in succession by the emperors of Byzantium to the princes of Kiev to salute the baptism of the Russian people. After the fall of Kiev to the Tatars (1204), the icon was transferred to the new capital of the Russian state, Vladimir— whence its title—and finally to Moscow in 1395, in order to protect the city from the invasion of the hordes led by the Tatar Khan Tamerlane, whose troops in fact inexplicably retreated from the walls of the city. After this miracle, over the course of Russian history, the icon of the Virgin of Vladimir was always considered the palladium and protectress of the nation.

According to the tradition, the virgin followed her Son all her life, whether at a distance, in his preaching first and then, close even physically, on the cross. The tremors, the fears, the pains of the Mother of God began with the birth of Christ and then from the flight into Egypt. In just this way her motherhood was called to increasingly become a sharing of the cross and hence of the redemption of humanity (page 91).

*A detail of the
"Vladimir
Madonna of
Tenderness,
With Scenes
From the
Akathist Hymn":
"The Flight Into
Egypt," sixteenth
century,
Moscow.*
DISTRICT MUSEUM OF VLADIMIR

THIRTEEN

MARY AND THE CRUCIFIXION

When the time of the life-giving passion arrived, and the merciful and sweet Lord was questioned by the chiefs and leaders of the high priests and was mistreated and crucified, the immaculate Mother not only never separated herself from him, but she suffered with him. I will say more, even if my observations may seem bold: she suffered more than he and took upon herself the pains of his heart: he, God and Lord of all, offered himself spontaneously in his flesh, while she found herself in the condition of human, feminine weakness; and she was filled with a total love for her most beloved and desirable Son. How, then, could the depth of her sorrow and lament be expressed, when she saw the suffering of the Impassible One and so deep a human passion? The divinely beautiful actions of Christ had already been performed, his innumerable miracles and his divine teachings and doctrine in his earthly life. Now nothing was lacking save for the fulfillment of the divine plan: the crucifixion, the burial, and the resurrection. Here we can see the sufferings and pains of the holy Virgin, greater than any word or thought. Here we can measure how far removed she is from all others. In fact, the time of the passion was then like a flame that devours the material: it burned all the others who abandoned him and fled; but it spared like gold the immaculate and blessed Mother, and revealed her as holier and more tested. Just in fact as her beloved Son and God, at the moment of his birth, revealed her to be both mother and virgin, so he preserved her as impassible at the moment of his passion: the blessed Mother was truly immersed in sorrow and suffered with him according to the order of nature, because above all of the love she nourished for him. But he made her impassible through the divine grace with which his soul was overflowing, and by virtue of the sovereign power that he showed in his Mother. [...]

That unique virgin lady, not used to the agitation of the people, and still less to a mob of thieves and armed soldiers and captains, went all about without fear, and never separated herself for an instant from her beloved Lord and dear Son, to remain always united to him in body and soul. She followed him from the moment he was captured till the fulfillment of his passion: she saw everything and listened to his words. [...]

The Blessed One, even if she found herself as if among serpents and asps, as if among wild beasts, an innocent dove or peaceful lamb, remained in the possession of wisdom, because she was overshadowed by the victory of her Son and Lord. She saw with her eyes and heard with her ears the accusations that they hurled at him; but in her mind she remained nailed to her sweet Son and to everything that he made himself undergo.

Maximus the Confessor, *Life of Mary*, TM, 2, 240

"I see him crucified and I call him king." Thus Christ appears in the icon (page 95), with open arms, his head serenely lowered with his eyes closed in death and his weightless body bent. The position of his legs accentuates a dance step, the dance of victory over death. Even in the most acute moment of the drama, Eastern tradition does not limit itself to presenting the realism of agony, but already lets the mystery of the resurrection shine through: "He has trampled down death by death."

The cross is rooted in the earth, "deep as a tomb," the tomb where lies the skull of Adam, the man who symbolically represents humanity waiting for salvation through the sacrifice of Christ.

The cross has three traverse sections: the lower one beneath the feet of Christ is usually inclined to continue the curve of the body, the line of pain; the side turned upward is meant to signify the destiny of the good thief, the "theological thief," who recognizes the Savior in the Man of Sorrows. The cross is the "balance scale of justice," the balance of human destinies now filled up by the sacrifice of Christ, which exceeds all human measure: no human sinner can ever make it swing definitively to the side of condemnation again. The Eastern Church lives the passion and death of Jesus by identifying itself with the good thief, who represents miserable and sinful humanity, though still certain of salvation and the victory of Christ. This certainty is likewise represented in the figures of the Virgin, Saint John, and the angels by a contained suffering, full of expectation of the resurrection.

"The Crucifixion," *fourteenth century, School of Moscow.*
ANDREI RUBLÊV MUSEUM, MOSCOW

WHEN YOU WERE CRUCIFIED, O Christ, all of creation saw and trembled.[1] The foundations of the earth were shaken by fear of your power. Today, at your exaltation upon the cross, the Hebrew people plunged into ruin. The veil of the temple was torn in two.[2] The tombs opened, the dead arose from their graves. The centurion saw the wonder and trembled;[3] but your Mother, standing near the cross,[4] exclaimed, groaning maternally: "How could I not weep and beat my breast!" O Lord, crucified and risen from the dead, glory be to you!

Today the immaculate Virgin, seeing you raised up on the cross, O Word, suffered in her bowels as a Mother, she had her heart bitterly transpierced, and groaning with pain from the depths of her soul, tore her cheeks, pulled out her hair, consumed by suffering. And so, beating her breast, she weakly exclaimed, "Ah, divine Son, ah, Light of the world! Why then have you set this before my eyes, O Lamb of God?" And the choirs of the disembodied angels, seized by fear, said, "O incomprehensible Lord, glory be to you!"

Seeing you hanging on the wood of the cross, O Christ, you, the Creator of all things and God, she who without seed brought you forth said bitterly, "My Son, where has the beauty of your face disappeared? I cannot see you iniquitously crucified.

"Hasten, then, arise, so that I too may see your resurrection from the dead after three days!"

Lauds for Good Friday, TM, 1, 932

1. See Matthew 27:45
2. See Matthew 27:51
3. See Matthew 27:54
4. See John 19:26

DO NOT WEEP OVER ME, O Mother,
seeing your Son in the tomb,
you who without seed has conceived in your womb.
I shall arise, in truth, and I shall be glorified
and I will raise incessantly to glory
those who exalt you with faith and with love,
because I am God!
The earth hides me because I wish it,
but the guardians of Hades tremble,
seeing me clothed with a bloodied tunic.
O Mother, by the blood of vengeance,
because I am God, I have beaten my enemies on the cross;
I shall arise again and I shall give you glory!
Let creation exult, let all the inhabitants of the earth rejoice!
Hades, the enemy, has been despoiled.
Let the women come forward with the perfumes;
I shall set free Adam and Eve and all their stock
and on the third day I shall arise!

Ode IX from the Canon for Holy Saturday

This composition (page 99), which unites the icon of Christ "Acheropita" ("Not painted by human hand") and the lament of the Virgin over the dead Christ ("Do not weep for me, Mother"), constitutes the supreme exaltation of the divine humanity, the artistic expression of the indissoluble link between the glory of the risen Christ and his humiliation in his passion and death. The intense and suffering expression of Christ dead in the tomb, the bare, understated profile of his features, the dramatic lament of the Virgin, and the pious ladies and the apostles, are balanced by contrast in the upper section by the grandiose and serene representation of the sacred face on the linen held up by the angels. In the lower section, the culminating moment of the mission of Christ is represented: the "Spouse" who consummates the marriage in the wedding chamber of the cross to generate redeemed humanity in his blood.

This composition has its traditional place above all on Holy Saturday, when the icon of the Bridegroom is carried in procession, and the people flock to kiss it to the singing of the troparion: "Behold the Bridegroom comes in the middle of the night, blessed is the servant whom he will find waiting; unworthy is the servant whom he will find negligent."

Against the gilded background, the body of Christ bears the attributes of the humiliation of his passion and death. This canonical type appears in the twelfth century, and from the end of the thirteenth century it is frequently found on icons, miniatures, and church walls, mostly alongside the altar. The Man of Sorrows, whom the Eastern Church also likes to call the "King of Glory," comes in the night of the human condition to take it upon himself and redeem it with his light. The unworthiness of man ("I see your adorned bride chamber, O my Savior, and I have no garment to enter it with. Make the garment of my soul to glow, Thou Giver of Light, and save me!") is redeemed by the life-giving blood that flows from the cross. The "new creation," the Church, is represented standing next to Christ in the figures of the Mother of God and of John the Evangelist, who share in his death in order to be made sharers in his resurrection.

We are faced here with the unity between the theme of earthly death and a fundamental principle of human life (which the Savior himself accepts), and the theme of victory over death by means of the cross as a fundamental principle of faith. The icon of Christ "Acheropita" appears as the standard that proclaims the glory of the resurrection achieved through the passion as sung in the troparion of the feast of the icon, which is solemnly celebrated by the Byzantine Church on August 16, in memory of the transferral of the icon from Edessa to Constantinople. Traditionally the icon served as a banner raised on the walls of the city, or by the troops in battle, to constitute the pledge of victory over the enemy, just as the cross of Christ is the victorious weapon over evil and death.

*"Christ
'Acheropita'"
and "Do Not
Weep for Me,
Mother," c.1570,
School of
Moscow.*
DISTRICT MUSEUM OF
KOLOMENSKOYE, MOSCOW

O MOTHER OF GOD, you are the spiritual paradise that, without being culti-vated, has brought forth the blossom of Christ: through him, the living cross was planted on earth.

Matins for the Feast of the Exaltation of the Cross

The significance of the icon (page 101) is played out entirely along the antinomy of cross-ressurection: while the Virgin has the facial expression, grieving and full of resigna-tion, that we find in the "Tenderness" type, the Child, at the revelation of the passion, has a moment of fear and, with a gesture full of confidence, clasps the hand of his Mother, as if seeking a refuge from the pain. The passion is foretold by the archangels Gabriel and Michael, who show Jesus the cross, the lance, and the sponge.

The archangels have their hands veiled, as a sign of adoration for the God-made-man, and in acknowledgment of the manifestation of God's redemptive power—that is, the cross is the sign of resurrection and the final victory. Furthermore, the gesture of the Virgin recalls the posture of the Hodigitria, who points to Christ, "the way, the life, and the truth." She consents to the sacrifice of Christ, so that man may be saved. Participating in the passion of Christ, Mary, the new Eve, becomes the Mother of all the living.

"The Mother of God of the Passion," *nineteenth century.*
PRIVATE COLLECTION, ITALY

FOURTEEN

MARY AND THE ASCENSION

In the first book, Theophilus, I wrote about all that Jesus did and taught from the beginning until the day when he was taken up to heaven, after giving instructions through the Holy Spirit to the apostles whom he had chosen. After his suffering he presented himself alive to them by many convincing proofs, appearing to them during forty days and speaking about the kingdom of God. While staying with them, he ordered them not to leave Jerusalem, but to wait there for the promise of the Father. "This," he said, "is what you have heard from me; for John baptized with water, but you will be baptized with the Holy Spirit not many days from now."

So when they had come together, they asked him, "Lord, is this the time when you will restore the kingdom to Israel?" He replied, "It is not for you to know the times or periods that the Father has set by his own authority. But you will receive power when the Holy Spirit has come upon you; and you will be my witnesses in Jerusalem, in all Judea and Samaria, and to the ends of the earth." When he had said this, as they were watching, he was lifted up, and a cloud took him out of their sight. While he was going and they were gazing up to heaven, suddenly two men in white robes stood by them. They said, "Men of Galilee, why do you stand looking up toward heaven? This Jesus who has been taken up from you into heaven, will come in the same way as you saw him go into heaven."

Then they returned to Jerusalem from the mount called Olivet, which is near Jerusalem, a sabbath day's journey away. When they had entered the city, they went to the room upstairs where they were staying. Peter, and John, and James, and Andrew, Philip and Thomas, Bartholomew and Matthew, James son of Alphaeus, and Simon the Zealot, and Judas son of James. All these were constantly devoting themselves to prayer, together with certain women, including Mary the mother of Jesus.

Acts 1:1–12, 14

AFTER HAVING CONCLUDED THE WORK of our redemption

and having united the things of the earth and those of heaven,

You ascended into glory, O Christ Our God;

you did not separate yourself from us,

you stayed with us forever,

and cried to those who love you:

"I am in your midst, and no one is against you."

Kondakion for the Feast of the Ascension

In the treatment of this subject, the artist clearly has in mind the New Testament story, the tradition and the spiritual meaning of the feast.

The composition (page 105) is divided into two strips: in the upper zone Christ rises up in the mandorla held up by two angels, while the lower part comprises the Mother of God and at her side two angels and the apostles. The link between the two zones is provided by the figure of the Mother of God, slender and elongated, vertically extended, isolated from the mass of the other figures through the white garments of the angels. Parallel to the kondakion of the Ascension, the icon stresses the union of earth with heaven, of humans with God, in the mystery of the redemption.

The Mother of God, at the center of lower section, is in the "orante" posture, absorbed in contemplation, in sharp contrast to the posture of the apostles, who point agitatedly to the sky, full of astonishment and consternation. The white color of the icon is a symbol of paradise, of the beatific vision; here the white background created by the garments of the angels indicates that the Mother of God is already participating, before all other creatures, in the glory of the Risen Christ. In her, "more honorable than the Cherubim and more glorious than the Seraphim," come together the earthly world and the angelic world, according to an analogy between the monastic and the angelic life that will be broadly taken up in Christian tradition.

"The Ascension," 1408, Andrei Rublëv, Daniel Chorny, and assistants.
TRETYAKOV GALLERY, MOSCOW

105

HAVING FULFILLED FOR US GOD'S PLAN of redemption, and having united the affairs of earth with those of heaven, you were taken up in glory, Christ, God, in no way separated but remaining without difference, and announcing to those who love you, "I am with you." [...]

Then, as ordered, the first line of angels announced to all the leaders on high: "Lift up the gates and open wide the doors, the heavenly and glorious doors, for the Lord of glory draws near. Clouds, strengthen your backs for him to mount; Air, prepare for him to travel through you. Heavens, be opened up; Heavens, the heavens of Heavens, receive him, since he comes to you who says, 'I am not separated from you; I am with you.'" [...]

The apostles, bowing down, gave adoration to God, and, full of praise, they let their voices ring out to the mountain, as though shouting in honor of Olivet. They said: "You have surpassed Mount Sinai; for it became the speaker's platform for Moses' words, but you, for the words of Christ. The former was the law; but the grace is in you.

"You who are without sin," said the apostles, "grant peace to us, and through us to your world, to the ambassadors of your mother, for the enemy does not endure seeing the fine things which have happened to us. Do not drive him away, he who says, 'I am not separated from you; I am with you, and no one is against you.'"

Romanos the Melodist, *Hymn for the Ascension, LIII*

WHICH TROOP OF ANGELS stood around you as you prepared to take a journey, accompanying your steps for miles? What would the leader Michael not do with so lofty a guide? What would Gabriel, the sacred messenger, not carry out? Or how would Raphael not go to help the nurturing Mother who bears you, thinking that this was a matter of the throne of God?

I believe that the one would wish to stretch his palms beneath your feet; the other, while beating his wings, would wish to cleanse the road again. One would create breezes to prevent the heavy heat from burning; the other would stretch his wings so that the rain would remove its waters. [...] The hovering troop of angels flies to prevent your foot from stumbling. If there are many vigilant troops, when you fall into a deep sleep or drowse off by yourself, you would lead them all to watch over you. O Virgin, thanks to your merits, you are wholly worthy of the celestial worship that is given you when the troop of divine choirs surrounds you. When you rise up, the sun itself would tremble with sacred respect; and the moon would ask to stand beneath your feet; the mechanism of the world would present you to its Maker and through your limbs it would admire God.

Venantius Fortunatus, In Praise of Holy Mary, TM, 3, 611

IT IS TRULY JUST TO GLORIFY YOU, O Mother of God, always blessed and wholly immaculate, Mother of Our God, you who are more honored than the Cherubim, and without comparison more glorious than the Seraphim, you who without corruption gave birth to the Word of God, we shall magnify you as the true Mother of God.

Hymn of Cosmas of Maiuma

Beginning in the sixteenth century, there is a marked increase in icons that translate the hymns of the Eastern Church into painterly terms. The link between icon and liturgy is always very close, since the icon reveals its peculiar significance through the liturgy and makes present the one who communicates himself to human beings in the eucharistic sacrament. This complex four-part representation (page 109) is an exposition of joy, a painterly hymn in praise of the Virgin, who is likened to the glorious humanity of the Son, with the echo of a hymn sung during the liturgy of Saint John Chrysostom.

The composition develops from the upper left: (1) "It is truly just to glorify you, O Mother of God." The Virgin is seated on a throne, surrounded by angels; below her are prophets and apostles, that is, the heralds and preachers of the gospel. (2) "Always blessed and wholly immaculate Mother of Our God...." The Mother of God is shown in full stature, in the manner of the "orante," surrounded by the prophets Elijah and Moses, and by monks and hermits, who invoke her as the most shining example of the vocation to virginity. (3) "You are more honored than the Cherubim, and beyond comparison more glorious than the Seraphim...." Here the Virgin is represented in the glow of the eight-sided star, which indicates the presence of the Lord of Hosts, and surrounded by all the angelic powers. (4) "Without corruption you gave birth to the Word of God; we shall magnify you as the true Mother of God": the mother of God is on the throne, surrounded by a crown of bishops and prophets, among whom are Cyril of Alexandria and Basil the Great: the priests who through the liturgy make present in the Church the mystery of the incarnation.

*"It Is Truly Just
to Glorify You,"
1550–1560,
School of
Moscow.*
CATHEDRAL OF THE DORMITION IN
THE KREMLIN, MOSCOW

FIFTEEN

MARY AND PENTECOST

I learned both what is secret and what is manifest,
for wisdom, the fashioner of all things, taught me.
There is in her a spirit that is intelligent, holy,
unique, manifold, subtle,
mobile, clear, unpolluted,
distinct, invulnerable, loving the good, keen,
irresistible, beneficent, humane,
steadfast, sure, free from anxiety,
all-powerful, overseeing all,
and penetrating through all spirits
that are intelligent, pure, and altogether subtle.
For wisdom is more mobile than any motion;
because of her pureness she pervades and penetrates all things.
For she is a breath of the power of God,
and a pure emanation of the glory of the Almighty;
therefore nothing defiled gains entrance into her.
For she is a reflection of eternal light,
a spotless mirror of the working of God,
and an image of his goodness.

Although she is but one, she can do all things,
and while remaining in herself, she renews all things;
in every generation she passes into holy souls
and makes them friends of God, and prophets;
and God loves nothing so much
as the person who lives with wisdom.
She is more beautiful than the sun,
and excels every constellation of the stars.
Compared with the light she is found to be superior,
for it is succeeded by the night,
but against wisdom evil does not prevail.
She reaches mightily from one end of the earth to the other,
and she orders all things well.

Wisdom of Solomon 7:21—8:2

The circular structure of the composition (page 113) is meant to underline the communion and unity of those who believe in Christ. The Mother of God and the apostles are seated in prayer, waiting for the Holy Spirit to descend upon them. The Spirit stands out on high in the form of a dove inscribed in two intersecting rhombuses (the cosmos and eternity), and surrounded by darting flames about to land on each of those present. In this way, the icon represents the Church about to be born, new humanity initiated by Christ, of whom the Mother of God (who takes the central position, usually occupied by the Savior at the Last Supper) is the Mother and the personification.

The prevailing colors in the icon are red and gold; in the descent of the Holy Spirit the mystery is actually fulfilled that makes man a son of God and sharer in the divine glory (always expressed in Eastern iconography by gold, the "color of colors"). The icon of the Virgin united with the apostles in the upper room in prayer while waiting for the Holy Spirit is thus, as the encyclical Redemptoris Mater *affirms, the icon of the unity of the Church, the icon of the new humanity to which our world, torn by divisions, longingly tends.*

*"Pentecost,"
nineteenth
century,
Russian.*
PRIVATE COLLECTION, ITALY

IT BEING THEN PENTECOST, they were seated, and the Paraclete came down from heaven, the guardian and sanctifier of the Church, the helmsman of those who voyage through stormy seas, the enlightener of the wandering, the judge of the competitors, and the crowner of the victors.

He came down to clothe the apostles with power and baptize them. The Lord says: "Within a few days you will be baptized with the Holy Spirit."[1] This is not a question of a partial grace, the power is complete. As those who are immersed in water are totally surrounded by the water, so they were baptized totally and perfectly by the Holy Spirit. But while the water is poured outwards, the Spirit baptizes the soul as well internally and completely. [...]

Lest the greatness of the grace that was descending remain unknown, a sort of heavenly trumpet sounded. "Suddenly a sound came down from heaven like a wind that blows impetuously,"[2] to signify the coming of him who lets men take the kingdom of heaven away with violence,[3] so that the eyes might see the tongues of fire and the ears hear the sound. "And it filled all the house in which they were seated."[4] The house became like the receptacle of spiritual water; the disciples sat within it, and the whole house was filled. Thus they were totally baptized according to the promise:[5] they were clothed in body and soul with the saving garment. "Then there appeared to them like tongues of fire, distributed and resting on each one of them. And they were all filled with the Holy Spirit."[6] They received a fire that does not burn, but saves, that destroys the thorns of sins, which makes the soul splendid.

Cyril of Jerusalem, *Seventeenth Baptismal Catechism*, in *"Le Catechesi"*
(Alba: Edizioni Paoline, 1966)

1. Acts 1:5
2. Acts 2:2
3. Matthew 11:12
4. Acts 2:2
5. Acts 1:5
6. Acts 2:3–4

O MOST HOLY LADY, Mother of God, light of my poor soul, my hope, my protection, my refuge, my comfort, and my joy: I thank you for having enabled me to be a partaker of the most pure Body and most precious Blood of your Son. Enlighten the eyes of my heart, O Blessed One who carried the Source of Immortality. O most tender and loving Mother of the merciful God, have mercy on me and grant me a repentant and contrite heart with humility of mind. Keep my thoughts from wandering into all kinds of distractions, and make me worthy always, even to my last breath, to receive the most pure Mysteries of Christ for the healing of my soul and body. Give me tears of repentance and thanksgiving that I may sing of you and praise you all the days of my life, for you are ever-blessed and praised. Amen.

Anonymous, *Prayer After Communion to the Most Holy Mother of God*, TM, 1, 920

O MOTHER OF GOD, you are the true Vine that gave the fruit of life. We beg you: intercede, O Sovereign, with the apostles and all the saints, that our souls may find pity.

You are hope, protection, refuge of Christians, an unbreachable wall, a tranquil port for the shipwrecked, O pure Mother of God. As you save the world through your unceasing intercession, so remember us as well, O Virgin worthy of praise.

You are the unbreachable wall of us Christians, O Virgin Mother of God; having found refuge in you, we remain invulnerable; having sinned anew, we have an advocate in you. Therefore we cry out to you in gratitude: "Hail, full of grace, the Lord is with you!"[1]

Prayer at the Third Hour, TM, 1, 924

1. Luke 1:28

The composition (page 117) represents a bold and powerful synthesis of Christian ecclesiology: the mystery present in the liturgical celebration, in the breaking of the bread of the apostles, as seen in the lower part (at the center we can make out Peter, whose billowing mantle recalls the breath of the Holy Spirit), is the same mystery that exists before time, awaited and made present in the Old Testament (the prophets who form the crown of the composition), incarnate in the person of Christ (represented here in the upper portion in the features of the angel of Eternal Counsel, the divine Sophia [Wisdom]), and perennially operating in the Church, of whom the Virgin represents the form and the apostles the foundation.

The historical dimension of the Church is indicated by the presence of the prophets and above all by the two Johns, the Baptist and the Evangelist, alongside Wisdom, who personify the two alliances, the Old and the New Testaments. But the cosmic, eschatological dimension is also very strong, suggested by the stars that the two Johns bear in their hands, by the presence of the heavenly hosts and above all by the representation of Christ as "Divine Providence," a rare typology that serves to point up the Wisdom-action of the Word, present in the Church through the Holy Spirit.

*A detail from
"Praises for the
Mother of God":
late sixteenth
century–early
seventeenth
century, School
of Stroganov.*
MUSEUM OF SOLVYCHEGODSK

WE SEE THE HOLY VIRGIN as a brilliant luminary enlightening those who live in darkness; for having kindled the immaterial Light, she leads us to the knowledge of God and fills our minds with radiance, so that she is worthily praised in these words:

Hail, O Beam of the Mystical Sun;
Hail, O Radiance of the Light without setting!
Hail, Lightning-Flash that brightens the souls;
Hail, Thunder-Clap that strikes down the foes!
Hail, for you have raised the many-lighted star;
Hail, for you have opened the many-coursed Stream!
Hail, O you who cleansed the stain of our sins;
Hail, holy Vessel overflowing with joy!
Hail, O Fragrance of the sweetness of Christ;
Hail, O Life of the mystical banquet!
Hail, O Bride and Maiden ever-pure!

[…] By singing praise to your maternity, we all exalt you as a spiritual temple, O Mother of God! For the One who dwelt within your womb, the Lord who holds all things in his hands, sanctified you, glorified you, and taught all people to sing to you:

Hail, O Tabernacle of God the Word;
Hail, Holy One, more holy than the saints!
Hail, O Ark that the Spirit has gilded;
Hail, inexhaustible Treasure of Life!
Hail, unshakable Tower of the Church;
Hail, unbreachable Wall of the kingdom!
Hail, O you through whom the trophies are raised;
Hail, O you through whom the enemies are routed!
Hail, O Healing of my body;
Hail, O Salvation of my soul!
Hail, O Bride and Maiden ever-pure!

Akathist Hymn, TM, 1, 960

SIXTEEN

THE DORMITION OF MARY

The Response of Dionysius the Areopagite, first bishop of the Athenians, to the request of Titus, bishop of Crete, about the passing and assumption of Mary, the holy Virgin Mother of God:

I make known to your brotherly sentiments, O noble Titus, that when she had to pass from this earth to the other world, that is, to the heavenly Jerusalem, nevermore to return; when she had to enter, according to the lively aspirations of the inner man, into the tents of the Jerusalem above, then the hosts of the holy apostles, according to the indications received from the heights of the great light, in conformity with the holy will of the divine order, were united in the twinkling of an eye from all the places in which they had received the mission to preach the Gospel.

Suddenly, they found themselves united around that glorious and virginal body. In that place they appeared as twelve luminous rays of the apostolic college. While the faithful stood around, she bade farewell to everyone, she, the holy Virgin who, drawn by the ardor of her desires, along with her prayers, lifted her most holy and pure hands towards God, raising her eyes, accompanied by vehement sighs and aspirations toward the light, toward him who was born from her womb, our Lord, her Son.

She gave up her all-holy soul, like perfumed incense, and entrusted it to the hands of the Lord. And in this manner, adorned with graces, she was lifted up to the regions of the angels and, like a shining burst of lightning, she was admitted to the unchangeable life of the supernatural world.

Suddenly, after that, among the groans mixed with laments and tears, amid an ineffable cheerfulness and hopefulness that came over the apostles and all the faithful present, that body, still alive, was lifted up above every law of nature, that body which God received, that spiritualized body, was piously recomposed, as befitted her who had breathed her last. It was adorned with flowers, amid a chorus of edifying hymns and brilliant discourse, as the circumstances required.

The apostles, inflamed by the love of God and swept up in some way by the ecstasy, lifted the tomb up with care in their arms; they lifted her who was the mother of light, according to the good pleasure of the lofty heights of the Savior of all. They deposited the tomb in the place destined for burial, that is, in that place called Gethsemani. For three consecutive days they heard above the place melodious airs of psalmody performed by angelic voices, and it was delight to hear them; but then nothing.

Now, then, in confirmation of what had happened, it occurred that one of the holy apostles was missing from their number at the moment of the meeting; he arrived later on and obliged the apostles to let him see tangibly the precious treasure, that is, the very body that God received, by opening up the tomb. Hence they were forced to satisfy the ardent desire of their brother.

But when they opened the tomb that had contained the sacred body, they found it empty and bare of the mortal spoils. Even though they felt sorrow, they managed to understand that, after the heavenly chants had ended, the holy body had been removed by the very ethereal powers, after having been predisposed in a supernatural manner to the dwelling of honor, of light, and of glory hidden to the visible and carnal world, in Jesus Christ Our Lord, to whom be given glory and honor for all eternity. Amen!

Pseudo-Dionysius the Areopagite, To Titus, TM, 1, 627

IN GIVING BIRTH YOU KEPT YOUR VIRGINITY and in your dormition you did not abandon the world, O Mother of God. You passed on to life, being Mother of life, and with your intercession you set our souls free from death.

A marvelous miracle! The fountain of life is placed in the tomb, and the grave becomes a ladder to heaven. Rejoice, O Gethsemani, holy dwelling of the Mother God! Let us acclaim her, O faithful, imitating Gabriel: "Hail, full of grace, the Lord is with you,[1] he who lavishes on the world, through you, his great mercy!"

O, your mysteries, O Chaste one! You appeared, O Sovereign throne of the Most High, and today you have been transported from the earth to heaven. Your glory sends forth rays of grace. Virgins, arise with the Mother of the King. Hail, full of grace, the Lord is with you, he who lavishes on the world, through you, his great mercy.

Let the Powers, the Thrones, the Principalities, the Lordships, the Cherubim, and the terrible Seraphim glorify your dormition. Let the sons of the earth rejoice, adorned with your glory. Let the sovereigns bow down together with the archangels and angels and let them exclaim: "Hail, full of grace, the Lord is with you, he who lavishes on the word, through you, his great mercy."

We, all generations, proclaim you blessed, O Virgin Mother of God; in you Christ Our God, the Uncontained, deigned to be contained. Happy are we who have you as our advocate: day and night you intercede for us, and the scepters of the kingdom are unshaken through your supplications. Therefore, as we sing hymns we call out to you: "Hail, full of grace, the Lord is with you!"

Explain to us, O David, what this present feast is? He answers: "She whom I have sung, in the Book of Psalms as the Daughter of God, maiden and virgin, has been transferred into the celestial dwellings by Christ, who was born from her without seed. For this reason, let the mothers rejoice, as do the virgin spouses of Christ, exclaiming: "Hail, you who have been transferred into the heavenly dwellings!"

The venerable choir of the inspired apostles was miraculously reunited to give glorious burial to your immaculate body, O Mother of God, worthy of all praise. With them sang the angelic hosts, hymning with reverence your assumption. This we will celebrate with faith.

In your childbearing, the conception had no seed; in your dormition, death was without corruption: you passed from miracle to miracle, O Mother of God. How indeed could she who has not experienced wedlock nourish in her womb a baby while remaining a virgin? How was the Mother of God swathed with perfumed spices as if she were dead? Therefore together with the angels we cry out to you: "Hail, O full of grace!"

Stichera for the Feast of the Dormition, TM, 1, 939

1. Luke 1:28

The composition (page 123) is clearly divided into two sections, an earthly zone and a heavenly one. In the lower area, behind the deathbed of the Mother of God, we see the Savior, who receives her soul, as in a sort of paraphrase of the representation of the Virgin with the Christ Child. At the side of the deathbed are the apostles, gathered together for the final good-bye to the Mother of God. They sadly lower their heads with a restrained sadness; almost all of them bring their hands to their throat or lips, as if to stifle a sob of sorrow and so as not to disturb the sacred silence.

Among the apostles, bishops are also depicted, with the crosses or the white "homophoria" (mantles) thrown over their shoulders. These are bishops who have in their own works described the event of the dormition of the Mother of God. On the left, we see James the brother of the Lord, who became bishop of Jerusalem, and alongside him Denis the Areopagite; on the right, Saint Timothy and Saint Jerotheus.

The upper section, in heaven, embraces in turn two distinct areas. In a splendidly golden heaven the apostles fly on the clouds, hastening to the ends of the earth to arrive at the bedside of the departed Virgin. Two angels point the way to the apostles; and two others, their hands veiled as a sign of veneration, stand by Christ without daring to draw near but remaining at a certain distance from him, so that around the form of Christ a sort of mandorla or halo is formed, the emanation of his divine energy.

At the top of the icon, a segment of paradise is represented, blue with golden stars, where an angel is bringing in the soul of the Virgin, while another, pointing out the way to her, incenses her.

*"The Dormition
of Mary,"
c.1200,
Novgorod.*
TRETYAKOV GALLERY, MOSCOW

The composition of this icon (page 125), painted by an artist from the circle of Theophane the Greek, is extremely laconic. The accent is placed on the mystery, through the prevailing blue (the sophianic color, par excellence) and the relief given to the candle lit before the deathbed of the Mother of God. The lit candle is, during the liturgy, an excellent sign of the presence of the mystery; apocryphal tradition relates that this candle was lit by the Virgin herself when the angel announced to her the coming of death. The bystanders are few and crowded together on the sides; in the center, the gigantic figure of Christ stands out. He solemnly supports, in the golden robes of the resurrection, the little white figure of the Virgin's soul. Above the Savior is a flaming cherub, symbol of the inextinguishable ardor of eternal life.

"The Dormition of Mary," last part of the fourteenth century, Moscow.

TRETYAKOV GALLERY, MOSCOW

125

IN YOU, O MARY FULL OF GRACE, every creature rejoices, the choir of the angels, the human race. Sanctified temple and spiritual paradise, glory of virginity, God took flesh from you; and he who is our God from all time became an infant. In your womb he made his throne and made your womb vaster than the heavens. In you, O full of grace, every creature rejoices; glory be to you.

Hymn from the Byzantine Liturgy

The Virgin is shown in her cosmic significance as the joy of all creation. In the background (page 127), paradise is represented by the temple, wrapped in luxuriant vegetation: it is the heavenly Church to which all the nations flow. On the first level, the Virgin stands out with the Child in her lap: the joy of the heavenly creatures is seen in the choir of angels which is spread around her, while, from below, the saints reach out toward her. We are facing a "spiritualized temple," put together by the beauty of love, by a motherly heart that gathers into itself the universe.

Among the blessed we can make out various orders of sanctity: the first one at the feet of the throne of the Virgin is Saint John Damascene, who offers her the scroll with the text of the hymn he composed, which supplies the title of the icon (and which also appears transcribed all around the frame of the icon, to underline its significance as a painted prayer). On the left we see the prophets, the Fathers of the Church, the Desert Fathers, and the just. On the right of the Virgin appear the apostles, the martyrs, male and female, and a group of nuns.

"The Joy of All Creatures," sixteenth century, School of Moscow.

ANDREI RUBLËV MUSEUM, MOSCOW

127

APPENDICES

*"Our Mother of
Perpetual Help,"
second half of the
fourteenth cen-
tury—beginning
fifteenth century,
School of Crete.*

CHURCH OF THE MOST HOLY
REDEEMER AND SAINT
ALPHONSUS, ROME

Our Mother of Perpetual Help

Perhaps one of the most popular and familiar images of Our Blessed Lady is the icon of "Our Mother of Perpetual Help," which is enshrined in the Church of the Most Holy Redeemer and Saint Alphonsus in Rome. Its iconographic style is that of the School of Crete during the second half of the fourteenth century or the beginning of the fifteenth century.

This icon rested in obscurity in various locations in Rome (brought there by a merchant who, according to legend, brought the icon from Crete to Rome) until it was given over to the care of the Redemptorists (the Congregation of the Most Holy Redeemer). The public display of this icon sparked a renewed interest in devotion to Our Mother of Perpetual Help. Under the aegis of the Redemptorists, devotion to Our Mother of Perpetual Help has spread to the four corners of the globe.

In this icon (page 130), the Virgin appears in a standing posture, dressed in a red tunic with long, tight-fitting sleeves, a dark blue robe, and a shawl of the same color. The shawl covers her head and falls over her arms and shoulders, but it allows her celestial blue veil which conceals her hair and part of her forehead, the red tunic at breast level, and the cuff of her sleeve to be seen. In the center of the head and on the shawl is a star with eight rays; a little off center one can also see a cruciform star with a blue center and gold highlights. The circular halo around her head has stippling and floral decoration that is typical of the Cretan School. The Virgin turns slightly towards her left. Her gaze is sacred and profound. It is not directed toward her Son, but toward whoever is contemplating her.

The child is shown with brown hair and childlike features and his whole body is visible. His head is turned to his left. His look is not directed at the archangel Gabriel (whose hands are covered with a tunic and which are holding a cross with three horizontal crossbeams with four black nails at his foot), but at a point outside the picture.

The Child is dressed in a green, long-sleeved tunic with a red waistband and reddish mantle. The mantle and tunic are covered in lineal, gold folds. He is wearing brown sandals with gold laces, but one sandal hangs loose and we are able to see the sole of his foot. The face and the whole figure of the child seem to express a great serenity.

Fabriciano Ferrero, *The Story of an Icon*, first English edition,
Redemptorist Publications, United Kingdom, 2001

INDEX OF BIBLICAL CITATIONS

INDEX OF ILLUSTRATIONS